COPING
WITH
THE CRISES
IN
YOUR
LIFE

This is My Faith
How to Preach to People's Needs
Understanding Grief, Its Roots, Dynamics and Treatment
Facing Ourselves
A Psychology for Preaching
You and Your Grief
The Pastor and His People
For the Living
Telling a Child About Death
Counseling the Dying (coauthor)
Understanding Prayer
Group Counseling
When Someone Dies

COPING
WITH
THE CRISES
IN
YOUR
LIFE

Edgar N. Jackson

JASON ARONSON
Northvale, New Jersey
London

To Estelle,
who has grown through
many crises with me

Portions of Chapter 3 originally appeared as an article, "Body Image and Grief Response," in *Religion and Bereavement*, New York, Health Sciences Publishing Corporation, 1972. Copyright © 1972 Health Sciences Publishing Corporation. The author gratefully acknowledges permission to reprint this material here.

New Printing 1986

ISBN: 0-87668-413-4

Library of Congress Catalog Number: 73-369

Manufactured in the United States of America

CONTENTS

FOREWORD

Two of the best kept secrets of the twentieth century are that everyone suffers and that suffering can be used for growth and "becoming." During the beginnings of the psychological revolution, starting with Sigmund Freud, there was a subtle and tacit assumption that if we could only learn the right principles and methods we would eliminate psychic pain from the human experience.

There is no question that our armamentarium of insights and therapeutic techniques does offer help and comfort, but we have begun to search for a new balance. We do have many new avenues for the relief of anguish, but the fact of being alive inevitably means the endurance of tragedy, the crises of life.

Coping with the Crises in Your Life is a practical, deep, and wise analysis of "the mysterious ingredient that makes crises into stepping stones." Edgar Jackson makes it clear that we are not at the mercy of the crises of our lives. We will certainly all face major crises (sometimes caused by our own actions), but how we respond to them determines their effect on us. Analyzing the anatomy of crises from a wide variety of aspects, Dr. Jackson carefully leads us to an understanding of the great range of human responses to crises and to a comprehension of how we can choose among them, how we can determine how we will respond, and how we will be affected. Will we grow through a crisis or become less because of it? Given the understanding presented by this book, the choice is—at least in large part—up to us. With a wealth of illustrations from his extensive experience, Dr. Jackson holds our interest, stimulates and expands it until we are hardly aware of how much our knowledge has grown.

Jackson is unquestionably the outstanding authority of our time on crisis management. Some years back I started a research project on the psychological condition of cancer patients and how psychotherapists might be of help to them. I looked for someone who could help me understand what happened to people under the hammer blows of such an overwhelming crisis. Of all those who had worked and written in the field, I found Edgar Jackson's approach to be the most human, meaningful, and practical.

But this is not the major issue—that he has written and lectured widely on this subject. What is important is that he is a man of profound humanity; he is a man who has suffered himself and has compassion for all others in the human condition. He has a rare combination of gifts. As an experienced psychological counselor, he is concerned with the healing of the personality. He is also a gardener of the human soul who has an infinite faith in the cosmic possibilities of human courage.

Lawrence LeShan, Ph.D.
Research Associate
Ayer Foundation

PREFACE
to the Second Edition

This book was the first effort to write a comprehensive introduction to crisis psychology. Since its first edition in 1974, interesting developments have taken place in the theoretical and applied aspects of psychological research and practice.

In psychology two newer disciplines have in the past decade attracted wide interest and professional support. Humanist psychology has become a viable alternative to behaviorism in the understanding of persons, while crisis psychology has provided a resource for helping people cope with life problems. In its more specific form the latter has been increasingly an addendum to medical practice. This is only natural, as the data of crisis psychology come largely from research in psychosomatics and psychogenics.

A decade ago holistic medicine was little known or understood. Now major medical schools have professors of holistic medicine or medical humanities. A team approach to the care of patients is now provided in pain clinics and stress management centers. Music therapy, art therapy, and forms of meditation and spiritual therapy are employed to help modify patient attitudes with the explicit purpose of modifying body chemistry and immunological resources from within and without.

Where a short time ago there was suspicion and open conflict among those who represented varied approaches to the needs of the patient, now there is increased willingness to share resources and broaden the base of human understanding and cooperative practice. This change in professional attitudes may be accounted for by a deeper understanding of how wider research and practice may be employed for common goals in patient care.

Communications from various places indicate that this book in its original edition was used in crisis management clinics and in training ambulance crews, seminary students, medical personnel, and others in the community who represent a first line of defense against traumatic experiences. The clear knowledge that crises are the internal response to external events may change the climate of human relationships when intervention is necessary. A new understanding of the importance of psychological first aid may have a profound effect on how people are cared for in emergency and other potentially damaging circumstances.

The continued research in cause-effect processes in illness points ever more forcefully toward the importance of wise management of crises and the stress that accumulates around crisis events. Crises tend to come in clusters and can feed upon each other with a major effect on the glandular systems which through chemical factors control the immunological resources of the body.

Many of the crises in life tend to be social and emotional rather than physical. One professor at an arts college wrote saying that if all freshmen were obliged to read this book during orientation week there would be a lot less sorrow and failure during this time of major adjustment.

It is with the hope that this book can be again useful to professionals, trainees, and those of the general public who would like to gain perspective on what is happening to them, that I welcome this new edition.

Corinth, Vermont
February 1980

COPING
WITH
THE CRISES
IN
YOUR
LIFE

1

You Face a Crisis

Life is filled with crises. Every time you have to make a choice there is a crisis, for you must decide which alternative to pursue.

We grow through crises. As we develop skills in making choices and living with them once they are made, we are better able to face the future.

But not all crises are the same. Some are small and easily managed. Others overwhelm us with the demands they place on our skills to adjust and adapt to new circumstances.

Students of crisis psychology have observed that crises are apt to be important turning points in an individual's life. Some people are broken by a crisis. Others grow and become stronger.

When a person is broken by a crisis, it appears that his inner strength and skills for adjustment are not adequate to meet a new and demanding life experience.

A person can grow through a crisis if he has developed inner strength and coping skills. This makes him feel stronger, more perceptive, and more competent.

Those who study crises have a major concern. If crises are so important for life, and the wise management of them so basic to personality development, how can we help people to meet crises so that they grow instead of finding themselves fractured?

In our exploration through these pages we will seek to learn as much as possible about the nature of crises, how they affect people, where they come from, and the light understanding can throw on them.

We will also look at various types of crises that seem characteristic of life's developmental pattern. We will look at the crises of childhood, youth, maturity, and special times of illness and bereavement. We will try to understand the resources available at different times of life to manage crises wisely.

Also we will try to assess the ways we can help ourselves or accept help from others in handling troublesome events.

At the beginning it may be wise to look at some typical and not so typical crises. We will look at two people who turned their crises into launching pads for great achievement. We will look at two people whose crises undermined their lives and seriously impaired their usefulness to themselves and others.

The first is Anne Frank. As a psychologist deeply interested in adolescent development, I have long been intrigued by this young girl's tremendous depth of insight and personal power.

I recently had the chance to spend a long, quiet afternoon with Otto Frank, Anne's father, in Basel, Switzerland. I plied him with endless questions about Anne, her training and development, and her character traits. Here is the story I pieced together from his words.

To her father, Anne seemed an ordinary child. She enjoyed playing with other children, did most of the things the other children did, and appeared to have no unusual traits that could mark her for greatness. She did well in her studies but was by no means brilliant. She did like to write.

When Hitler came to power, the family moved from Germany to the Netherlands and for a time felt secure there from the ravages of nazism. But with the coming of Seyss-Inquart, the Nazi commissioner of the Netherlands, life for Jews in Holland became increasingly difficult. Finally, the means of escape were shut off and those who could went into hiding. The Franks retreated into an attic room over a business establishment and were provided for by friends who smuggled food to their hiding place.

Then the changes in life pattern became critical. Absolute silence had to be maintained from early morning, when the first workers came into the rooms below, until the last workers left in the evening. Usually this time of silence lasted ten or twelve hours. Try to imagine, if you can, being absolutely quiet for all the daylight hours. This meant refraining from moving about, for one step might make the floor boards creak. It meant no one was to talk, to laugh, to sob, or to sneeze. It meant all life had to be frozen into the most rigid forms of self-control.

Under these threatening conditions, what would happen to life? People need to communicate, but here the restraints on communication were stringent. To maintain her emotional health, Anne had to develop alternate modes of communication. On her twelfth birthday her father had given her a five-year diary. Each page gave limited space to record events, thoughts, and feelings.

Driven into silence and surrounded by all-pervading fear, Anne turned to her diary as a point of reference where her inner being could find expression.

Day after day Anne sat in silence, listening to her deepest thoughts. She wanted to write them all down, but she could not for the space was limited. So she had to sort out her thoughts to record only the best.

Teenagers tend to explore their own deep feelings. They feel they are unique, that no one has ever felt the same way before. The urge to seek meaning for life, to build a philosophy of life, is strong. This natural impulse plus the compelling events around Anne Frank came together to create a remarkable response.

Anne apparently asked herself discerning questions about herself, her motives, her concerns for life. She asked herself questions about other people and what drove them to be kind or brutal. She looked beyond surface behavior to try to understand people's motivations. She asked the questions and then, in the quiet terror of her brutal separation from normal life, tried to find the best answers possible. Her life became a quest for meaning in the apparently meaningless. Her sensitive spirit had to develop a philosophy of life large enough to sustain her in her ordeal as day after day added stress.

Out of her crisis Anne created a mature and beautiful self that showed in what she wrote. Now, a long generation later, young people are inspired by what she discovered. Other people caught up in life crises are helped by her insight. Suicidal people take a new lease on life, and defeated people gain the courage to try again. Threatened people learn how to take the hazards of life and turn them into resources for growth. Anne's authenticity shows through. For her, the crisis led to creativity.

Quite the opposite was the case with Paul Williams (not his real name). He came to me late one Saturday evening in a state of anxiety and distress. Here, in brief, is his story.

Paul was a sales executive for a large corporation. For twenty years he had been a district sales manager for his company, constantly waiting for a promotion. Two weeks before he had been promoted to eastern regional sales director, which meant he was in charge of sales for the entire country east of the Mississippi River. Since receiving the promotion he had become increasingly restless, with sleepless nights, increased irritability, and feelings of greater stress with each new day.

When Paul came into my office, he looked haggard and anxious. In response to my queries he gave some clues to what was going on inside him. Promotion in his company was dependent on death or retirement. At meetings of the district sales managers there were constant jokes about health and age. Paul admitted that he had often sat through sales meetings jealously watching his superior for any signs of failing health or clues to retirement plans.

Paul said that the next week he faced his first assignment as chairman of a sales conference. As he put it, "I will be the focus of those twenty pairs of eyes and I know what will be going on behind them. They will curse me and my luck for being promoted over them. They will be carefully hiding their jealousy but I'll know it's there. All of their drive for promotion will show in their eyes as they look at me and wonder when I'll die or how long it will be before I retire. And I can't face it."

Hostility, resentment, and jealousy are often the byproducts of competition. How can people learn to manage the crises that come with intense competition? Paul was willing to give up even before he started on his new assignment, not because he felt incompetent but because he felt so threatened by the fruits of the implicit conflict in the struggle for advancement. He said, "You know, right now I'd rather be back at my old job than face that bunch next Wednesday. I've been where they are. I know what they think. With all the good humor and camaraderie that shows on the outside, deep inside they will all wish I'd drop dead. I can't take it."

As Paul explored the roots of his anxiety, it became clear that he was so afraid of death that his fear constantly interfered with living. He said he had often felt he would die before he had a chance at promotion. He was quite sure his colleagues were centering their thoughts and energy on wishes for his death. He would wake up at night and see himself at the head of the table with all eyes focused on him. He imagined what the various looks meant, and that compounded his anxiety. Although we tried together to examine his fears and reassess the looks and attitudes of his colleagues, we were never able to completely resolve his death anxiety.

Paul did face his colleagues and try to function in his new assignment, but with his state of mind it would probably have been better if he had not. Before the next year was over, he had died of a heart attack suffered on the way to his office. He was acting out the inner conflict that wanted and did not want the promotion he had received. The energy of life was used up in the stress of this inner crisis. Instead of producing something valid and valuable out of his crisis, he added to his misery and hastened himself toward tragic and untimely death.

Death anxiety can certainly be used more constructively. Margo completed her rigorous training in medical school with

honors. She went through the never-ending crises of her training sustained by the idea that someday she would be able to heal
disease and help save lives.

When she had completed her internship, Margo sought out
a remote section of the West Virginia mountains where there
was no physician for miles around. Here she set up her practice.
The people were poor and the chance of becoming a well-to-do
doctor was remote, but Margo was happy to be where she was
so obviously needed. Almost immediately she had good rapport
with the mountain people and a position of importance in their
lives.

Day after day she treated their ills in her office with its
limited facilities. She traveled to their homes where she prescribed for their needs and offered comfort and love. Wherever
she went she had a feeling of self-esteem and usefulness.

Then one day she was summoned into the hills to assist a
mother with childbirth. She went as far as she could in her jeep
and then climbed farther up to the remote hamlet where the
patient lay. As soon as she saw the young woman, Margo was
aware that she was in extremis. She had lost most of her blood
in hemorrhage. Through heroic intervention Margo saved the
baby, but the young mother died as she worked at the hopeless
task of preserving her vital functions. Then what happened?

Let's use Margo's own words as she related her experience
to me. "I remember taking the baby out the door and placing
it in the arms of one of the women standing in the yard. I looked
around into their piercing eyes and found myself unable to
speak. I walked through their midst and down the trail toward
the spot where I'd left my jeep. But I didn't see it. I just kept
on walking. I must have walked twenty miles before I began to
come to my senses. My feet were blistered and bleeding. I was
so completely lost I had to ask where I was. I finally begged a
ride back to my office."

Margo went on with the story. "When I was back in my office
I sat for hours, stunned. I began asking myself questions. What
had happened to me? Why had I gone to pieces? What did it
mean for my career as a physician?

"I knew I couldn't go on with the practice of medicine until I'd come to terms with whatever it was inside me that had to be dealt with. I did a minimum of work for a few days as I struggled for perspective. I talked my experience over with colleagues and friends. I finally decided that I would have to go back to medical school and do some of the unfinished work of my education. I had to learn to cope with my feelings. So I did advanced work in psychiatry and psychotherapy, first of all for myself. Then I expanded my awareness of the fact that much illness is the result of fear, anxiety, and guilt. So I set to work to cope with these things in myself and then in others."

Margo went through a crisis and faced its meaning with determination. She grew through it to become a better equipped and more effective physician. Instead of retreating from the fact of her inadequacy, she accepted it as a challenge to her feelings of omnipotence and power over the lives of others, and a clue to her own source of weakness. She did not run away from herself. Instead, she fought her way to personal victory over her anxiety, and also to greater competence as a physician.

The fourth person we look at was not as skillful in facing a crisis. Alex was sure that he was looking forward to retirement. He had worked hard in a steel mill for more than forty years. A widower, he had raised his family and now felt he could relax and enjoy the ease and comfort he had earned.

For the first month he visited some of his children in nearby states. Then he took the first long trip he had ever taken in his life, to visit a daughter who was a member of a missionary order in South America. The first two weeks there were delightful, but then he became restless and wanted to go home. It was as if his vacation was over and he had to get back to work.

When he was home again, he puttered around the house for a few days making minor repairs, but soon he became restless again. Then one morning he rose early and went down to the factory gate. He said to himself that he just wanted to visit some old friends. But when they hurried on into the plant and left him standing alone outside, he was overcome with a strange feeling of anger and uselessness. No one seemed to care much that he was there. After a few more mornings with the same results, he felt he would try to spend the noon hours at the factory. Again the results were the same: He was ignored. A few quick greetings and he was alone.

Alex seethed with resentment and felt cheated. All his life he had found meaning for his existence through his work, and now he had no work. He became moody and developed aches and pains. He became self-centered and irritable. He wrote his daughter in South America to say that he was ill and no one cared what happened to him. If she wanted to see him before he died, she would have to come home at once. She was thrown into confusion for her life work was in jeopardy. She loved her father, but she also loved her vocation. She was given a temporary release from her work and returned to her father. A complete medical examination failed to show any organic cause for the maladies of which he complained. He was miserable and made everyone around him as uncomfortable as he was by his unreasonable demands.

Alex could not face the crisis of aging and retirement. He mismanaged his crisis so that it projected crises into the lives of others. Instead of making retirement a time of fulfillment with relaxation and new interests, he made his retirement a calamity for himself and everyone near him.

Four crises happened to four people. A teenager, a young professional woman, a middle-aged businessman, and an aging factory worker met threatening events in quite different ways. How different were the results! For two the crises led to creativity and a new capacity for growth. The nature of the crisis was not changed, but it was used to bring new and richer life.

But Paul and Alex met the crises with despair, anxiety, and maladjustment. Instead of growing, they became reduced persons, a source of misery to themselves and certainly no help to those they claimed to love. On the other hand, Anne and Margo faced their crises with conscious and unconscious determination to make whatever life brought them an opportunity to develop a better self. Instead of being overcome by their crises, they marshaled their resources to rise above them.

The same or similar crises can do vastly different things to different people. What determines whether a crisis happens to you or whether you happen to the crisis?

2

The Nature of a Crisis

All crises are personal—they happen to people. People have the feelings. People have the involvement. People have the human encounter and the emotional capacity that makes a crisis a significant event in one's personal history.

But what is the stuff of which the crisis is made?

As individuals we become what we are through a never-ending process of communication and relationship. We are bound up with other people in every aspect of our lives. Before we are born, we live inside another person and all that happens to her in some way happens to us.

When we are born, we are related to other people in dependency, in emotional development, and in family structure. No matter what happens to us, we are in a process of discovering ourselves and our true nature.

We call this a process of achieving identity. Actually our identity is a feeling for ourselves that we acquire out of the feelings that we discover other people have about us.

Psychologically speaking, identification is much the same as love. When we identify with someone, we become a part of their life and what happens to them also happens to us. If something good happens to them, we feel good about it. When parents love a child, it is difficult for them to separate themselves from the events of the child's life. If the child is happy, they feel happy.

If the child learns to walk, they feel pride in the achievement. When the child learns to talk, they feel a personal sense of accomplishment. Growth is shared growth, and joy is shared joy.

But not all experiences of identification are pleasant. The identity relationship can lead to an identity problem. When a child becomes ill, the parents may actually suffer more than the child. When a child is injured, the parents feel the injury. The emotional investment of one person in the life of another creates vulnerability. He is apt to be hurt by anything that hurts the person he loves.

When two persons have a strong emotional tie, they may feel doubly injured when there is misunderstanding or conflict. When in a moment of irritation or anger a person speaks thoughtlessly to one he loves, injury occurs and it produces guilt on one hand and pain on the other.

When an identity problem is raised to its highest degree, we have an identity crisis. When something devastating happens to a person we love, we can be devastated. Here the personal crisis can be most painful. A friend falls in a skiing accident and is paralyzed, and we feel the pain and injury as if it were our own. A loved one is killed, and the tragic and untimely death may disorient our lives for months to come. The intensity of the identity relationship tends to determine the degree of personal injury we suffer when someone close to us suffers.

Erik Erikson has done extensive research on the nature of the identity crisis. He finds that these crises emerge from three types of human experience.

First is the loss or threatened loss of somebody who is important in our life structure.

We can immediately think of a variety of conditions involving this form of acute deprivation.

A youngster starts off for his first day at school and his mother watches at the door as he is engulfed by the school bus. A child who has been central in her constant concern for years is now separated from her by a circumstance she cannot easily control. And the youngster looking out the bus window is aware of inner confusion and a loss of security. He has a strange feeling of separation from what he has known.

This experience of insecurity in the face of change can be repeated many times in childhood. Changing schools, going from an elementary school to the more remote and unknown precincts of junior high school, can have the same threatening sense of loss and dislocation.

The same kind of feelings can develop when a youth moves out of his home to attend college. He moves into a new world with a freedom he wants but does not want. His parents also have a new freedom, but it may not be welcomed. They may be concerned about the things that can happen in the new environment where old ways of living are lost and old securities are no longer present. This can be the stuff of which crises are made.

Certainly this loss or threat of loss shows up when a person is critically ill with the possibility of all the changes that may come with death. Our security system is closely bound with the people who make us feel loved and secure. It is threatening to think of living without them, or to actually have to make the adjustments that come when they are no longer there.

Sometimes this sense of loss comes with moving from one locality to another. This is especially true for children whose world of experience is relatively small. For a child, a move may change nearly all the known points of reference for life and may be more threatening than adults usually assume, for their own base of operations for living is much broader.

Divorce or separation also bring the type of loss that dislocates the individual's security system. Even if old ways of doing things were painful, they have been so deeply incorporated into life that they leave significant empty spots when they are gone.

So times of loss, or even the mere threat of loss, can well be the raw material of which crises are made.

Erikson says that crises are also apt to develop at the point where new and threatening people or events are injected into life. What are the characteristics of such potential crises?

Taking a new job may be threatening. Almost at once you are thrust into a place where everyone else knows what he is doing. They also know each other and you are the outsider. The new person has to learn a thousand and one things about life in a new setting, as well as face the looks and implicit judgments of people who think of him as new, a stranger, a person to be explored before he is accepted. For anyone limited in self-confidence, this can be a disturbing experience.

Getting married can produce a crisis. For people who have lived their own lives, made their own choices, and kept their own confidences, the need to share all of life and its decisions with new intimacy and total commitment may call for more instant skills than we have developed or possess.

Often the first year of marriage is fraught with stresses and conflicts that may be fatal to the relationship. Sometimes the events of the first few days or weeks may be so upsetting that the relationship never quite survives the first painful encounter.

What is true of marriage may also be true of childbirth. When I served as head of a psychiatric clinic for children and their parents, I was forced to become aware of the difficulty many women have with the obligations of parenthood. The seemingly fragile and utterly dependent creature puts stresses on the life of a mother and may create deep anxiety. Again and again, young mothers had trouble with breast-feeding because their anxiety produced glandular reactions that could actually disturb a child's body chemistry. When this happened, there was a build-up of anxiety and it could lead to serious repercussions in the relationship. The emotional threat that underlay the anxiety had to be worked through before the relationship could be made secure for mother and child.

Often illness injects people into new and threatening relations that compound the emotional effects of the illness. Apprehension about the physician, the meaning of the tests, and the implications of the illness for all the rest of life can be painful and distressing.

One day a few years ago I felt a pain in my chest that bothered my breathing, especially when I breathed deeply. So

I stopped at the office of our friendly family physician to see what he thought of the matter. He listened with his stethoscope for a few moments and then went to the phone, called the hospital, and requested a bed immediately.

When I protested, my physician cast aspersions on my soundness of mind and said that I was walking around with pneumonia. I drove my car to the hospital and parked it. Then I went into the admitting office, expecting to chat informally with old friends. But now there was a difference. A strict formality prevailed. For several minutes I answered questions about my parents and grandparents and the causes of their deaths. A mood of expectancy was created. Everything that had ever affected my health was explored and recorded. People were moving into the private areas of my life with a new and threatening authority over me.

When I had finished answering a number of relevant and apparently irrelevant questions, I was led into the corridor where a sweet little old lady with a wheel chair asked me to sit down. This assault on my feelings of strength and self-respect was almost more than I could manage. I looked at her and said, "Oh no, *you* get in." However, I was immediately overruled by the admissions officer. Once signed in, I must abide by the rules of the hospital. To make sure patients were clearly separated from visitors and to meet insurance requirements, they must be under the constant supervision of hospital personnel. So I hung my head and let the sweet little old lady, a volunteer, wheel me into the elevator and inquire solicitously about my well-being.

Much of my life had been spent around hospitals, but never as a patient. Always I had been armed with the authority that goes with professional status. Now all of this was stripped from me and I was obliged to face a completely new set of circumstances and human relationships. Soon I was wheeled into the pediatrics wing of the hospital. When I protested, I was told this wing had the only private room available at the moment. In a few moments a pretty young nurse handed me an outlandish piece of attire with the order to get out of my clothes and into its scanty protection.

I had been in bed but a few moments when the young nurse entered with a hypodermic needle. In business-like fashion, she turned me over and thrust some medication deep into the major muscle system of my body. From that time on I was no longer the person I had been. Instead, I was a pliable, compliant inhabitant of a world of vague feelings and limited comprehension. I had been delivered body, mind, and spirit into the hands of my physicians. I was a completely dependent and defenseless creature surrounded by those who exerted authority over me.

After a week of this treatment, I began to understand in a new way the difference between being a professional and being a patient. All of life was brought under the influence of new and threatening persons and circumstances. Even my capacity for consciousness and judgment was taken over. Whenever a person is hospitalized, it is reasonable to believe that in addition to the illness that sent him there he is also experiencing the multiple crises that emerge from his encounter with new people and conditions that modify his normal mode of existence.

Yes, personal crises do not come solely from loss or threat of loss. They can develop from the events that inject new persons and new authorities into life. More than we may at first realize, adjustments to a large variety of major and minor changes may accumulate into the material from which crises are made.

The third place where Erikson finds crises developing is the point where we experience changes in status and role relationship. Here any number of life events can contribute to the crisis.

When a person has been a student for years in the sheltered environment of the academic world, it is a major change to finally accept a degree and move out into the environment that is going to test all the training. When a brilliant young man received his Ph.D. in the morning and committed suicide that night, relatives and friends could not understand it. How could he do such a thing, just at the moment when all his years of study and personal achievement had been rewarded by his degree? The critical point in life for him apparently came when he was forced to change his status from that of the perpetual student to that of the professional, exposed to a world of demanding peers with no protection against his deep feelings of inadequacy and insecurity.

In Chapter 1 we looked at the case of Alex and his response to retirement. Here the change in status and role relationship was expressed not only through his retirement but also through its meaning for him. Up to the time of retirement his life had been worth living because of his work. Apparently he could not find meaning for his existence apart from industrial activity.

Similarly, in Chapter 1 we looked at Paul, who was faced with the threat of change in his status and role relationship. Instead of being fulfilled through promotion, he was afraid of it. His fear grew into uncontrolled anxiety that took its toll in his life. Being thrust into new responsibility and functioning with changed status may be threatening to an individual and create a crisis in his life.

Fred C. had always thought it would be satisfying to be called "Dean." When he was given a chance to accept administrative control over the faculty of his college, he accepted with pleasure. Things went along well when it was merely a matter of presiding over faculty meetings to consider curriculum items. But when charges of misconduct were brought against some of his close friends and he was obliged to carry out disciplinary action, his stomach ulcer began to cause pain. The only other time this had occurred was when he had been promoted to sergeant under battlefield conditions in Korea. When he had to decide who would go on patrol, he felt a tightening in his stomach. Now he was the "sergeant" for the faculty and the old ulcer showed itself again. The crisis that came with responsibility and change of status was getting to his insides.

Much the same thing was upsetting Mary S. When her husband died, she was mature and competent and seemed to be managing with personal adequacy. But as the months dragged on, she found that being a widow was different from feeling grief. Now she was functioning with a different lifestyle. She could not share in the activities of the couples she had known, for now she was the odd number who never seemed to fit. She did not want pity or special consideration, so she began to withdraw from the circle of friends she had known. There did not seem to be another group toward which she could move socially. So she became lonely and depressed. Her change in status was not just becoming a widow. It was the change in her relationships that produced the crisis she could not cope with.

Whenever life forces us into new and different roles, we may face critical readjustments. From preschool to school, from child to adolescent, from student to teacher, from wife to widow, from employee to retiree, from colleague to supervisor, from friend to antagonist, the changes that occur produce the inner stresses from which crises grow.

We can readily see how these changes in life bring conflict and stress. Any one of these problem areas can present stresses that are difficult to manage. But what happens when more than one or all of the critical points that Erikson mentions come together at one time?

Many of the major crises of life are multiple. When death occurs, there is not only the real loss but also the changes that force us to face new people and new conditions as well as new roles and a changed status. These are the points where it is important to grow in understanding and discover the help we need to manage crises that might otherwise destroy us.

3

The Importance of Crisis Management

We have looked at the nature of the crises that can impair life. Now we must understand why it is important to learn how to manage our crises. This will lead us to another level in understanding how crises originate in the depths of the personality.

Efforts to understand more clearly what takes place in crises has led to interesting psychological research. Because crises involve the deepest feelings and the most profound emotional responses, they are not easily understood. They are so basic a part of life that they are comparable to mother love and self-preservation.

Dr. Robert Fulton, author of the book *Death and Identity,* has helpfully moved us one step of the way toward understanding what is involved in crises by his efforts to illuminate the concept of identification as it relates to self-image and body-image. In its broadest meaning, identification is synonymous with love. When you love someone, you enter into his thoughts and feelings and value him as you value yourself. His feelings become your feelings. When he is injured and suffers, you are injured and suffer also. When he feels joy and satisfaction, you also feel joy in his joy and satisfaction in what satisfies him.

The processes by which identification takes place are rooted in the individual's sense of self, but they are fulfilled in the realization that the social self is never completed until it has significant relationships with other living beings. These relationships use a wide variety of experiences to enrich and deepen the interpersonal processes of life. Friendship, interests shared mentally, physically, and spiritually, common activities, and emotional fulfillment are the grounds from which identification develops.

But in order to understand the fullest meaning of identification, we have to move a step backward in the emotional processes, for our capacity for identification with the life of another is based on the nature and development of our own body-image. A person who hates his own body would find it difficult to show respect and love for the body of someone else. Rather, his self-hatred would tend to produce the perverted emotions of sadism, to seek to injure the body and feelings of another and find enjoyment in that emotionally rooted assault. Similarly, the person who values his own body and treats it with respect would find it quite reasonable and natural to value, enjoy, respect, and love the body of another person.

As emotional crises are bound up with our capacity to love, and our love is rooted in our body-image, we must ask: How does one develop a body-image? How does a healthy body-image enrich our response to life? How does an unhealthy body-image complicate an individual's life and make it difficult for him to cope with the powerful emotions released by acute deprivation?

Psychiatrists have been working for years to understand the origins and nature of body-image. They have developed a variety of theories related to it, and some of them may be useful for our exploration. The psychiatrist tries to understand what is going on in the mental and emotional life of his patients. In order to develop this insight, he examines the influences that shaped their mental and emotional life. When he finds a number of patients with the same cause-effect factors at work, he tends to develop a theory that explains what he observes. Let us now look at some of these theories for the light they throw on the concept of body-image.

Years ago Sigmund Freud, in his effort to unearth the roots of emotional disturbances, tried to understand how certain ideas and responses were planted in life. He surmised that young children were more sensitive and impressionable than most adults assumed. The general attitude of his day was that children were not able to learn much until they were old enough to talk and reason. But his clinical experience seemed to show quite the opposite, for the emotional patterns of life appeared to be quite well set while children were young, and many emotional responses seemed to be acquired before a child could talk.

In his effort to elaborate his theory on the acquisition of mental and emotional characteristics early in life, Dr. Freud gave prominence to an idea that should have been obvious but was largely overlooked: that children at an early age are completely dependent upon others, have strong feelings, and not only are sensitive to the feelings of those around them but also are singularly vulnerable to the feelings of others because they have not yet developed any forms of protection against emotional assault.

For instance, a baby that is dearly loved and the center of tender and loving attention will tend to become emotionally secure and feel a sense of his own value, not in words but in feelings. When he is sung to, cooed over, and affectionately snuggled to his mother's breast, the baby develops feelings about himself that are accepting and good. But if the opposite is true and the child is treated with disgust, neglected, handled roughly and without love, that child will probably show anxiety, insecurity, and other symptoms of hazardous feelings about himself. Feelings planted in the early stages of life tend to condition the emotional responses for all of life, and the child will be either anxiety free or anxiety ridden, self-confident or filled with feelings of inferiority, depending on the emotional climate of his early years.

These deep and early feelings about oneself are the substance of which the body-image is built. Freud said that "what is laid down inside is an image of what is perceived outside." Memory is not dependent upon recall, but may well be built into the emotional responses of life at such a basic level that the result is almost an automatic response to new experience. Freud spoke of this as the "body ego," but for more ease of comprehension it is now generally referred to as "body-image."

This body-image is an internalized amalgamation of a person's accumulated unconscious, preconscious, and subconscious experience. The anxious and insecure tend to draw from this reservoir of experience the type of response that shows up in defensive behavior. Others draw from the same reservoir the responses of self-acceptance and creative confidence that presume their past experience of security and acceptance by others.

Let us illustrate the way this psychological principle manifests itself in human behavior. A well-known actress was considered exceedingly beautiful, so much so that she was featured in moving pictures, photographs, and on magazine covers as the epitome of feminine attractiveness. But the way others saw her did not conform with her own idea of herself. Her early life had been marred by poverty, family discord, family breakdown, and the ensuing experience she interpreted as rejection. When the whole world acclaimed her as a sex symbol, deep within herself she felt unwanted and unacceptable. Her self-image and her body-image were quite different from those others attributed to her. So powerfully did these deep inner forces influence her life that she was unable to relate the acclaim to herself, but rather responded to the strong negative self-image. The victory of her inner negative image was so complete that ultimately she could not tolerate the self she had to live with and so, apparently, obliterated herself. The unhealthy self-image and body-image that had been built up in preverbal life experience seemed so dominant that they overwhelmed the later experiences that brought a completely different form of group response to her as a person.

Quite in contrast is the experience of another prominent actress. She is not particularly beautiful, in fact rather plain-looking. But she comes from a background of culture and security, emotionally and socially. She has never known a time when she was not valued as a person. In early life she was wanted and loved. Her first years were marked by warmth, love, security, and an all-pervading sense of her own personal worth. Now that she has been a successful actress for decades, she shows the inner durability of a person who can handle stress because her self-image and body-image are healthy and tend to correspond with the feelings other people have of her. The strength of her inner being is at work for her, rather than against her.

These contrasting illustrations may oversimplify the matter of body-image, but they do point out one thing that is crucial. That is that the body-image becomes an important resource for wise and healthful living. When the body-image is marred in early life, it can create emotional hazards that can plague every new venture. But when the body-image is sound, rooted in self-acceptance and group acceptance, and in clear correspondence with reality, it becomes a resource for meeting whatever life may bring, whether it be moments of joyful acceptance or times of acute emotional crisis.

As the depth and significance of feeling in life are related to the individual's feelings about himself, we can see how healthy feelings about the self tend to produce more healthful emotional responses to and relationships with other people. The roots of these feelings were enunciated by Freud and elaborated by some of his disciples. Their theories show how the attitudes of adults toward their life impulses and death anxieties become important factors in the unconscious response of their children toward life and death. Once planted, the emotional problem may persist through the years.

The following case illustrates this point. John S. was referred to me by the dean of the eastern theological school from which he was about to graduate. The dean said John had a deep fear of death and funerals that could impair his work with bereaved people. When I talked with John, I learned that although he had never been to a funeral he felt a sickening chill when a funeral coach drove by and would walk blocks out of his way to avoid passing a funeral home. John's father had been killed in an industrial accident when John was two years old. He had been told nothing of the event, but could not be protected from the emotional turmoil that surrounded it.

As he was an only child, John's mother was overprotective and actually clung to him emotionally to fill the void left by his father's death. John had been close to his father, and the only idea of death to him at his age was one of painful deprivation. Because he was so young, there was no clear distinction between physical and emotional pain. The word death, or anything that reminded him of it, produced an immediate and diffused response of discomfort. His response, copied after that of his mother, was to try to avoid the verbal and visual stimuli that caused the unpleasant response. His body-image was confused with that of his father. Since his mother would never answer his questions or discuss the matter, it became even more anxiety creating. His body-image was so involved in his grief for his father that he had never been able to make a clear separation between the two.

The process of counseling sought to bring the confused emotional processes to the surface so they could be discussed and sorted out. On this basis a new understanding developed, and John was able to separate his own basic feelings from the event that involved his father. In essence, he was able to free himself from the physical pain of his father's death. When that was done, he moved beyond the threat involved and was able to separate the death of an individual from the generalized anxiety that surrounded death as a persistent threat to his body-image and self-image. Then he was able to see other people and their needs in such a way that he could move beyond his inner problem and perform his pastoral duties wisely and well.

This case illustrates the condition that exists when a person is so completely identified with another at the level of body-image that he is overwhelmed with the pains of grief and the threats to selfhood. In effect he reexperiences the death over and over, and he has little or no protection against the distressing feelings that are continually related to the fact of death.

Only when the person is able to move beyond his own body-image to see with certainty that the death has happened to another and not to him, is he freed from the anxiety, the physical pain, and the emotional hazard that accompanies the confronting of the fact of death as a most acute form of deprivation.

Another way of illustrating the powerful emotional force related to body-image or body-identification is found in that complicated but basic drive we call mother love. We recognize that there is no human relationship in which the body-identification of one person is so close to another as in the process of gestation. This is doubly significant, for gestation tends to fulfill the powerful drives of sex and at the same time produce new and significant feelings between mother and child. The mother often finds meaning for her existence that she cannot find anywhere else. In fact, she may be able to value her body only when it is engaged in the procreative process. As one physician put it, "For many women, it is only when they are pregnant or breast-feeding that they really value their own bodies and know how to love themselves—for it is only by identifying with the child that they feel worthy of love."

This makes it possible for us to understand the powerful emotions of loss and despair that often appear at the death of a young child. More significantly than we are apt to realize, this loss diminishes the meaning of life for the mother. The strong body-identification is fractured at the point where it brings together several powerful emotional drives. In consequence, this fracturing process is one of the most difficult to cope with emotionally, not only because it must contend with important unconscious and instinctual drives but also because it tends to threaten the value structure of the persons most acutely aware of the critical loss.

Two psychological theoreticians have tried to develop their theories with a special interest in the mother-child identification and its relation to the self-image and its basic constituent, the body-image. Let us examine their insights.

Otto Rank was a student of Freud, but he felt the base of

Freud's theories was not broad enough. In his clinical observation Rank found what he felt was a significant correlation between the easy birth and the well-adjusted individual on the one hand, and the difficult or painful birth and the anxiety-ridden and disturbed individual on the other. He reasoned that the individual's first experience in his independent existence was the event of birth. While the event might not be remembered consciously, its marks were deeply impressed on the physical and emotional life of the developing person. A painful first experience in life tended to make the growing infant enter each new situation with apprehension and dread. And according to Rank, those born by Caesarian section, with little or no discomfort and no typical birth distress, moved easily into new events of life, free of the emotionally defensive stance.

Whether or not we accept the full implications of Rank's birth trauma theory, we cannot easily escape the fact that the nature of the birth may have a profound effect upon an individual's life. If such an early experience can so affect the concept of selfhood, it is not difficult to see that other powerful emotional events in early childhood can have a significant bearing on how the personality meets life crises.

Nandor Fodor, a Hungarian psychoanalyst, has carried the theoretical process one step farther backward by suggesting that the psychic communication between the unborn infant and his mother is a major factor in creating the self-image and its constituent body-image. According to Fodor, if the mother resents the conception and hates the unborn child, the fetal being has no protection against such hatred and is born with a backlog of low self-regard. If, on the other hand, the child is desired, planned for, and deeply loved in anticipation and in fact, this too will show in the feelings of self-acceptance and self-regard that shape the individual's emotional life.

Again, we do not need to accept the full implications of Fodor's theories to have a new sensitivity to the forces at work at the earliest moments in the individual's life to shape the feelings about the self and the body within which the self resides.

Students of accidents consider them meaningful forms of behavior. Unconscious drives toward self-injury make it quite clear that there is a reason why a major portion of accidents happen to a small minority of people. A faulty body-image and an urge to injure the self, which is most clearly reflected in the body and its feelings, may well explain more self-destructive behavior than we are aware. Karl Menninger, in his book *Man Against Himself,* points to many of the direct and indirect methods men employ in acting out their deepest feelings about themselves. Many of the mildly self-destructive habits and behaviors we often observe may be persistent expressions of feelings against the self at the point where the body is the focal point of self-awareness.

We have looked at the two questions we raised: How does one develop a body-image? How does the healthy or unhealthy body-image enrich or impair the individual's ability to cope with life experience? We come now to the nub of the issue. How does the body-image show itself in the way an individual meets and moves through the crises in his life?

The basic feeling that one has for his own body is acquired at such an early age that it is not usually subject to rational interpretation. It is made up of deep feelings that emerge from the reservoir of preconscious, subconscious, and unconscious experience. Therefore our understanding of it must take into account forms of behavior that do not appear reasonable or rational. But we do not discount these feelings for we have learned that all behavior in meaningful. Where it does not at first appear to be so, we are merely invited to look more deeply and carefully for the hidden meaning.

Because anxiety about death brings us face to face with some of the deepest emotions of life, much of the behavior we observe at such times has to be probed deeply to perceive and understand its meaning. In fact some behavior involves compensations so powerful that the things we see mean quite the opposite from what we would at first assume.

Perhaps the point at which we can best understand the dynamics of this process is not with total death but with the experience of what we might call partial death. This is observed in the phenomenon called the "phantom limb" sensation. When a soldier is so severely wounded that amputation is needed, he may experience the phantom limb response. I have interviewed many men in emergency military hospitals and have heard complaints about pain in the nonexistent limb. The process at work seems to be that the complicated nerve center that for a long time controlled the body part's activity continues to respond to nerve stimulation. It feels pain in the nerve endings. The portion of the body that continues to function cannot at once divest itself of the activities and sensations that related it to one of its parts, now missing. It cannot at once relate itself to the new reality of body-image, and so must engage in a rather lengthy withdrawal of sensation until the body-image conforms with the body-reality.

Paul Schilder, in his concept of body-image, uses the phantom limb theory to interpret the dynamics of adjustment and points out that with time amputees have a sensation that their phantom limbs shrink in size before completely disappearing.

Marianne L. Simmel of Brandeis University has recently made a careful study of these phenomena. She confirms the theory that the body-image develops slowly over long periods of time, and also that it tends to be more dependent upon past experience than present reality for its function. When she interviewed 27 persons who had been born with a limb missing, she found no evidence of the phantom limb phenomenon. For 18 patients with leprosy, where a portion of the body was slowly wasted away, the body-image had a chance to conform with the body-reality and there was no phantom sensation. She also found that the accumulation of experience tends to fortify the phantom sensation, and that amputations in young children did not produce as much of the phenomenon as when the limb had been used enough to become a significant part of the total body experience. Her conclusion is that it is not simply the existence of the limb but also the memory of sensations coming from it that make it a persistent part of the body-image. The body-image does conform to reality eventually, but it takes time.

It has long been realized that the crises of acute deprivation have many of the characteristics of an amputation. In my book *Understanding Grief* I wrote, "Bereavement is an amputation of a part of the emotional structure of life, and the use of tears may help to wash away the separation." Just as the nerve endings may at first have difficulty in relating the fact of the body-sensation to the modified body-image, so the person who suffers acute loss may at first be so involved emotionally that it is difficult or impossible to separate the body-image of the living being from the imagined sensation of death in the lost love object. Much of the feeling of pain that comes with the onset of acute grief is the feeling of emotional amputation in the life of the bereaved person. While one cannot easily imagine his own death intellectually, he can be so identified with a love object that in its death he feels a diminishing of his own life.

Coping with emotional crises is basically the effort to reorganize one's damaged self-image and body-image so as to begin to function in terms of reality rather than in terms of overidentifications that now have no foundation in reality.

Some interesting light has been thrown upon this process through a study of unwed mothers and their reactions to the loss of their babies through adoption. This study by William E. Lamers, a California psychiatrist, divided a group of teenage girls into two groups based simply on whether or not they had seen their babies. Dr. Lamers says that the girls who saw their babies, identified with them, expressed their love for them, and accepted their reality as independent beings were able to really give their babies up for adoption. While they had emotional pain, they were able to work through it because they were dealing with reality, not illusion, with fact rather than phantom.

Quite the opposite appeared to be true of the mothers who were persuaded not to see their babies at all. They appeared to be filled with diffused identity feelings that persisted for years. They wanted to look into every baby carriage, question every mother with a child, and in other ways carry on the tasks of their unfinished emotional separation. While the mothers who knew what they were giving up moved toward the establishment of stable marital relationships with families they could keep and love, those who tried to give up what they had not faced or accepted had difficulty in establishing the more normal and productive forms of human relationships.

It seems from Dr. Lamers' study that it is necessary to face the reality of a relationship in order to cope with it realistically. In both the phantom limb and adoption studies we see the impact of an emotional crisis on behavior. Our major question now becomes one of determining what can be done to prevent the more disturbed forms of reaction or reduce the degree of emotional injury that comes with acute crises.

It appears that crises can best be managed when they are anticipated and emotional preparation can be made. When the amputee could approach the crisis gradually, there was less reaction than when it happened without warning. It seems clear that with anticipation there can be a defensive stance. The unwed mothers who faced the reality of their children were in a better position to respond to counseling than those who had diffused their identity relationship throughout life rather than bringing it into sharp focus. It is apparent that for most people there are wise and unwise ways of moving toward crisis.

In fact it seems that the ability to develop wise ways of coping with emotional crises as they occur develops resources that can be employed in new and different times of threat and personal disaster. People can learn to measure their crises and gain skills in managing them. A healthful attitude toward the self, the body-image, and the rest of being gives inner strength that can stabilize a person when life is turbulent and strengthen his inner security when outer circumstances are most threatening.

4

Why Understanding Is Important

Knowing what is happening inside yourself during a time of crisis may help you through it. When you know why you feel as you do, even the disturbed feelings become less threatening. In this chapter we will try to learn how insight can be useful in self-understanding.

At the outset, though, we must face the fact that insight may provide only part of the solution. Some insight may be so intellectually isolated from the rest of life that it not only does not help but may actually be deceptive in making a person place his confidence where it serves no useful purpose.

Often a person in psychotherapy will have the feeling that he understands why he feels the way he does, but that it does not help him change the fact that he still feels that way.

When deep feelings are inaccessible to insight, it may well produce what we call "impotent insight"— an intellectual defense against feelings that are too painful to honestly confront or too deeply buried to reach.

But having admitted that there are sometimes such feelings at work within us, it is our purpose here to look at the positive insight we can have about the crises of life so that we can begin to develop some skills in wisely managing them.

We will examine two prevalent emotions that often lead us

into crises to see if our understanding of them can make it possible to gain some control over them.

Often problem areas are so close to us and so common a part of life that we fail to recognize them as hazardous. So we remove them from careful examination and let them continue to cause us trouble. In fact we grant them privileged status in our lives as the things we cannot really do anything about. The first of these is anger.

We all feel angry at times. We assume it is a part of our disposition to have angry feelings. We explain that some people are more easily angered than others because of their basic nature or land of national origin. We speak of the hot-tempered Irish or of "getting his Dutch up." The more we use these generalized excuses for anger, the less apt we are to really look honestly at our anger and what we can do about it.

Anger almost invariably starts with frustration. We are restrained from doing something we want to do and we begin to seethe inside. Before long we burst into explosions of hostile action. A child has an impulse to run free and is soon held back by those who are concerned about his safety. He does not understand the hazards of highways but he does feel the frustration of being thwarted in his desire for freedom. His response is to cry or yell or throw a tantrum. For this he may be punished, and in many instances the punishment is a further restraint of his freedom: "If you don't stop that immediately, you can go to your room and stay there." The anger builds up, and when it cannot be expressed directly it accumulates in a repressed form of resentment that may be easily triggered by any real or imagined threat to freedom of action.

The frustration that is the cause of anger may be specific and clearly seen or it may be generalized and difficult to bring into focus. A youngster may explode with anger when he is prevented from doing what he wants to do, and cause and effect are obvious. But an adult may show his anger in more subtle ways and be puzzled by his own behavior. There may not be a clear cause and effect relationship in what was said and his exaggerated response. It may well be that he is acting out of his reservoir of repressed anger and needs to understand what is at work to protect himself from himself.

John, who in his more balanced moments was a firm believer in women's rights and women's liberation, could not quite understand waves of strong feeling that flooded over him at times. Certain things his wife said would cause him to explode and he would be amazed to hear himself saying things like, "I'll show you who's boss around here, and if you don't get it through your thick head you'll get a poke in that thing you call a nose." And when his wife began to cry he would have a feeling of helpless rage that made things worse so that at times they might not speak for days. And all the while John felt ashamed and puzzled and angry at himself.

With insight he began to see that he was reacting to frustrations in his early life and was saying things to his wife that he had long wanted to say to his mother but never could. And crying only made things worse for him because this was another kind of action he could not cope with and so he became more frustrated. Until he understood the roots of his anger, it kept causing painful crises in his life. Until he could use his insight to develop new ways of acting toward frustration, he would not be free of old tensions that could break out in new situations.

Before one can begin to manage crisis-creating anger, it is important to admit it for what it is. Often we see the signs of it in common language. A person will say "I'm furious" or "I'm livid" or "I don't know when I have been so outraged." But then almost immediately the person will try to justify the angry behavior by blaming someone for causing his angry reaction. It may be that other people are stupid, negligent, or irresponsible. As long as we blame our anger on other people, we will be unable to cope with whatever it is deep inside of ourselves that produces the angry explosions.

In trying to bring this troublesome emotion under control, there are four things at least that need to be done.

The first is to admit that you are angry. This is usually the more difficult part of the process for we do not like to admit that our emotions could be out of control. We usually give a lofty motive to our anger. We may say, "I'm not angry, but some-body around here has to be concerned about what happens." Or, "There's a place for righteous indignation and I've got plenty of it."

As long as a person justifies his anger, he is not in a good position to understand or control it. As soon as he is willing to step back and look at his behavior objectively, he is in a position to do something constructive about it. A professional ball player with great talent as a pitcher was back and forth between the majors and minors for several years. The reason given was his uncontrollable temper. In the major leagues his opponents knew that he lost his control of the ball as soon as he got angry, so they made sure that he had something to be angry about. They ridiculed him and cheered when he made a mistake, and in short order he was knocked out of the game. Then he "got wise to himself." He admitted that he could not afford to lose his temper. He practiced self-control, and when he learned how to manage himself he stayed in the majors for several years with an excellent record.

After admitting the anger, it is important next to examine and analyze it carefully. Here you can ask yourself a number of direct questions: What makes me angry? When am I most apt to explode with anger? Are there special things that set me off? When I look at this anger closely, can I find anything in my background that could trigger it? Why do I allow myself to get so angry when I know what it does? Why do little things produce such a big response when the big things don't set me off nearly as much?

Honest answers to questions of this kind can lead to some greater understanding of where the anger comes from and why it shows itself the way it does. With this personal information it is possible not only to avoid the conditions that produce anger but also to eliminate some of the emotional energy that goes into anger. You can defuse your own explosives by understanding why they are unnecessary.

But having admitted and examined the anger, it is necessary to go a step further and set up methods for attacking this self-destructive mode of action. Sometimes it is as simple as saying, "When I feel myself getting angry, I will count to ten slowly," or "When I feel an explosion coming on, I will step back and watch myself and then decide whether or not I can afford to lose my temper," or even "When I feel a rage developing I will go and look at myself in a mirror for a while to see if I can stand what I see."

Some people may want to take a more sophisticated look at their problem. Instead of merely talking to themselves, they may want to use each new onset of the powerful emotion to do a laboratory exercise or a case study of their feelings and actions. They can walk away from the situation that bred the rage and go off by themselves quietly to look at the whole process that was at work—the other people, the external events, the internal responses. Then when they have put all these factors together, they can probably better understand what was going on and be in a better position to forestall it in the future.

Finally, they should be able to understand the angry behavior so well that they can decide they do not need it any longer. It can be jettisoned in favor of more mature, more rational, and more productive ways of acting. Or as psychiatrist Leo Madow says, in his book *Anger,* "Proper recognition, understanding, and channeling of this ever-present emotion can change your entire way of life, making it more comfortable, more productive —even prevent serious illness."

But having moved along this far, we realize that the powerful energy that goes with anger cannot just be dismissed. While it is important to understand what is going on inside a person, it is also important to learn how to wisely use the powerful emotions that are a part of life. What can we do with anger and rage as powerful emotional forces in life?

What can be destructive at one level of behavior can be used constructively at another if we learn how. There are at least four things that we can do with anger to make it productive rather than disruptive.

When anger is turned outward, it can hurt other people and damage our human relations. When it is turned inward, it can do us harm. Many types of organic disturbance can be traced to the effects of internalized anger. Trying to control such powerful feelings can produce high blood pressure, stomach ulcers, and heart malfunction. When an individual becomes angry with himself, he can produce a state of depression, and the more depressed he becomes the more angry he may feel, until he digs a deep pit for himself and has real trouble getting out.

There are better things to do with anger. The anger and its energy can be diverted. Anger generates energy that must be handled wisely. Usually this can be done by using up the glandular secretions and the muscular energy in other ways. Lots of wood has been chopped by the energy of anger. A long walk may be a reasonable substitute. Actually any large-muscle activity can be of use in working off the energy of rage.

But perhaps the best way to handle the emotion of anger is to prevent it from getting out of hand at the beginning. If you see other people for what they are, individuals like yourself, struggling to cope with their powerful feelings, you will not be so apt to let them get to you. When you understand your responses as well as the meaning of their behavior, it may well be that you will not need to feel angry at them or yourself ever again. So self-mastery becomes an end result of insight and understanding. Crises can be prevented before they start, and problems of life can be anticipated and managed by developing new skills of personal and social understanding and control.

The second of the emotions that can cause no end of difficulty in personal relations is jealousy. Jealousy is an irrational form of behavior that usually emerges when one person feels threatened by another because his sense of security with a third person is jeopardized. Usually jealousy develops in relation to someone we love, or some position of status we feel may be lost. This can be in relation to employment, political position, or social preferment. At any point where your security is threatened by another, you can feel the seething of jealous feelings. Usually jealousy is so unacceptable a feeling that it is not admitted as such. Jealousy may show up as self-pity or as manipulativeness. Because of its insidious nature, jealousy can poison human relations without producing any valid benefits for anyone.

When Mary saw the new girl who was employed as a secretary in the office, she had deep and sickly feelings. She could not say just what it was that made her feel that way, but her discomfort was real and damaging to her. She found herself comparing the physical attributes of the new secretary with her own, and always to her disadvantage. She compared their personalities. She watched the new secretary's every act and attitude, especially in relation to the men who were her employers.

Mary found herself highly critical of the new girl and even lay awake nights thinking about her and her challenges. Mary began to feel insecure in her own position even though her term of employment was much longer and her personal record was excellent. Finally in the long hours of the night she began to examine her feelings. "I am jealous and that doesn't really make sense. Why should I be jealous? If I got to know her, I might get to like her. Perhaps I should try." So she set up a plan of action. She invited the new secretary to lunch. She learned about her interests, her life, her goals, and soon found that her fears were unwarranted. Instead of a threat, Mary found a new friend who enriched her life.

Jealousy can be one of the least productive emotions we can develop. Yet it is a constant threat of life especially at the points where we feel insecure. If we do not really love ourselves and feel inadequate, we can suspect that others do not really appreciate or love us. Then we make ourselves vulnerable to the wild imaginings that grow from our fears and suspicions.

Like anger, jealousy is a powerful emotion and it can be used to complicate or destroy the lives of those who hold the feeling as well as those against whom it is directed. Mature and self-confident people seldom feel this form of threat from others. But many of us have weak spots in our personalities, and it is in these vulnerable spots that our irrational feelings take root.

But like anger, jealousy can be brought under control by

ordered steps of insight and evaluation. First it is important to accept the jealousy for what it is and name it honestly. Then it is possible to examine what the conditions are within the self that make this emotion possible. What weakness or uncertainty about one's self leads to this feeling of inadequacy and fear? How can it be examined and analyzed so that it can be seen clearly both as to its roots and its expression? Then how can one attack the inadequate behavior and put something more logical and sound in its place?

Most of the crises we have in life are centered in other people. But many of the causes for crises are found within ourselves. Developing an understanding of what we project into our human relations can make it possible for us to eliminate many crises before they develop, and to manage those that have developed more wisely. If we assume that every problem has a solution and that in most instances we are a major part of the problem, we have moved a long way toward accepting the insight that we can use to manage the crises of life more soundly.

5

The Anatomy of Crisis

People are often mystified by their behavior at the time of a crisis. Something deep within them seems to take over. What they say and do has qualities they do not recognize as part of themselves.

These mystifying forms of behavior are almost like an automatic pilot. The direction of life appears to pass from clearly conscious and rational forms of control to ways of action that are powerfully motivated but whose sources are obscure.

Sometimes the response in crises reveals great strength. A person may run faster, jump higher, endure longer, and see more than normal. His whole being seems to be fortified from some inner reservoir that he is not usually aware of, and during the crisis he is a different person.

At other times the response may produce a collapse of normal functioning. The physical system may run out of control with nausea and vomiting at one end and a loss of sphincter control at the other. The respiratory system may be out of control with gasping and sighing. The heart may race as if it were completely out of control. The muscle system may let one down as it is overcome with weakness. The consciousness may be temporarily blotted out with a spell of fainting.

We are obliged to ask: What brings about these major

changes in the way a person functions organically in time of crisis?

Perhaps if we look more closely at a specific instance of behavior in crisis, we will understand something of the dynamic factors let loose.

A tour bus ran at high speed into a sand truck loaded with many tons of sand and gravel. The accident took place on a well-traveled highway near a business center, so many people were nearby. People were quickly divided into two groups largely related to their learned skills. A physician whose office was nearby was almost immediately doing heroic tasks of emergency relief for the injured. A policeman was immediately concerned with unsnarling traffic and rerouting it so that emergency vehicles would have ready access to the point where they were needed. A newspaperman was immediately at work getting names and addresses and detailed information concerning persons involved in the accident. Others became engaged in assisting the doctor and the police in rendering emergency aid. However, some persons near the scene who observed the blood, the injuries, and the dead bodies reacted in quite different ways. Some were merely curious and complicated the problems by their curiosity. But others fainted and collapsed, thus adding to the problem. What made the difference?

Those who explore behavior in catastrophic events have discovered that the more people who can be put to work to do constructive things, the better off they are. As long as they are busy, they are using up energy with a sense of direction and this keeps them from being overinvolved with their own inner responses to the external conditions. This tends to postpone the personal response until a time when there is more perspective and more inner control. Why would this tend to be so?

Here we are obliged to look at some basic elements of our anatomy, for we have inner mechanisms that start to function when there is a major threat to life.

Deep in the center of the brain is a small region known as the diencephalon. It is an enlarged section of the spinal nerve at the point where it enters the major area of the brain. It is in front of the medulla oblongata, underneath the major portion and yet incorporated in the thalmic region. It is almost completely surrounded by the cortical region of the brain.

The diencephalon is the most primitive region of the brain and is shared by many other creatures with a highly developed nervous system. It has a significant place in the evolutionary development of the brain, for it is entrusted with the mechanisms related to self-preservation. With the development of man's mammoth brain, there has been a long and slow process of encompassing the basic diencephalic responses with much cortical adaptation. This is where learned behavior and rational judgment have modified the basic organic responses.

For instance, when the receptors—the sensory equipment by which we experience the environment—are activated, they receive signals and transmit them to the brain. The capacity for reason then evaluates the messages and decides on a course of action. The bridges that connect the primitive region of the brain with the highly developed portion of the brain that controls reasoned response are at work to decide what muscles will be employed to react to the stimulus.

But in some circumstances this connecting equipment that relates sensory response to reason is interfered with, and at times completely fractured. This usually happens when the important primitive functions entrusted to the diencephalon are interfered with so that the connecting bridges with the rest of the brain are made inoperative. Then nonrational and spontaneous self-defensive behavior may be observed.

What are the important functions entrusted to the diencephalon, and what interferes with them?

The diencephalon is from early times in the evolutionary process entrusted with the complicated mechanisms that have to do with the sustaining, preserving, and protecting of life itself. These life defense functions are so important that they are provided with emergency powers that can produce reactions without having to engage the rest of the brain with the time-consuming processes of evaluation and reason. The impulses from the sensory equipment may race to the top of the spinal nerve and if the situation seems to warrant it, the activators, the muscles, and glands can be immediately put to work without the rest of the brain being involved.

The important functions entrusted to the diencephalon have to do with hunger, thirst, sex, and self-defense or self-preservation. As we can imagine, these can be closely related to many areas of crisis. But the civilized person is usually able to control these functions unless there is a powerful triggering event or process that sets the defense mechanisms to work.

The stimuli that can set the diencephalic processes in motion usually have to do with intense pain or prolonged frustration. The study of starving persons indicates that there may be major changes in patterns of behavior affecting human relations and normal civilized modes of relating to others. Intense pain also may trigger defensive or offensive action that is well out of the norm.

Let us look more closely at the way these mechanisms work. We can see it in the response of the animals that we have, over long periods of time, domesticated.

In our home we have a cat called Emily. She is a lady-like creature, quite refined in her habits and affectionate in her attitudes. It is interesting to observe the way she responds to the stimuli that are related to her diencephalon. This quiet and gentle creature is transformed when she sees a mouse. She becomes alert and poised for action. The ancient hunter deep within that was essential to life-support breaks through the thin veneer of civilization. Every sense and every muscle is alerted for attack, and she becomes a killer.

Other stimuli also can quickly change Emily's personality. She likes to sit in my lap but that is not always convenient, so when I push her off she takes up a place under or near my feet. If the phone rings and I jump up to answer it and inadvertently step on Emily's tail, she goes through a rapid change of personality. The quiet and gentle creature lets out an awful squawk and I may quickly have a claw sunk into my ankle. She almost immediately feels apologetic and we go through a period of explanation and adaptation to the mild crisis. The pain she felt triggered an instantaneous defensive action that was out of character, but the cause and effect factors were clearly understandable.

Emily can also respond to threats to her security system. If another cat is introduced to the household, she will become inhospitable, emit threatening noises, and show herself to be deeply disturbed by the presence of competition. Her jealousy is set in motion by the defensive mechanisms of the diencephalon at the point where her security system is assaulted.

If changes of this kind can be observed in a cat, we can perceive something of the mechanisms at work and their power in causing modifications of human behavior.

The instinctual drives toward the preservation of the species are as powerful and significant. Angus is a well-bred Labrador retriever, strong of body and a graduate with honors of a course in canine manners and discipline. But twice a year he forgets all about his education and undergoes major changes in his loyalties and willingness to respond to his master's commands. These times always coincide with the periods when a female dog three miles away is in heat. Even a strong chain that attaches Angus to the barn may not be adequate to restrain him when the strong impulse for racial survival takes over. His heightened sensitivity, his sense of purpose, and his personal endurance seem to make it easy for him to pull the metal fittings off the barn and drag his long chain across country to make his rendezvous with canine destiny.

When we realize that these same powerful forces are buried deep within the anatomical equipment of every human being, we can sense the possibility not only for the response to crises but also for the response that creates crises.

When a person experiences acute physical or psychological pain or persistent frustration, the stimuli may be so intense that there is a breakdown of the bridges to the areas of cortical adaptation and the raw diencephalic behavior may break through. What does it look like in human beings?

Civilized responses to the hunger impulse can lead to formal dinners, banquets, family meals, gourmet cooking, and membership in a cookbook club. Much that is good in life can center around the refined pleasure of eating.

But when normal eating patterns are frustrated, the results may be devastating. In illness, in famine, in the confines of a prison camp when food is not available, there may be a release of primitive instincts that lead to fighting for food, stealing of food, and a variety of devious acts designed to satisfy the selfish interests of the hunger-ridden person. Even the deviant behavior of the hunter during the hunting season may reveal behavior that expresses primitive urges rather than civilized concerns. A recent news report said 40,000 acres of the Everglades were aflame in roaring fires destroying millions of feet of valuable cypress trees. The cause of the fire was attributed to hunters who wanted to destroy the underbrush so hunting would be easier. Such destructive and nonrational behavior cannot easily be separated from the primitive impulses set in motion by the racial memory of hunger and the desperate needs for food for survival.

Compulsive thirst is not something reserved for people lost in the desert. Millions of people in our culture are in almost constant crisis because they have perverted their basic mechanisms of thirst by subjecting themselves to an artificially stimulated thirst for a habit-forming depressant drug called alcohol. Life disruption, personal malfunction (especially in automobiles), social dislocation, and familial destruction are crisis-producing in the lives of untold numbers of people. The problem cannot be separated from its diencephalic roots as a self-applied form of therapy designed to satisfy deep frustrations by employing the basic sucking and drinking mechanisms so essential to sustaining life in young children.

One does not have to be a marriage counselor to be aware of the multiple crises that are let loose in life by the primitive drives of sex. Freud centered much of his theory of neuroses and therapy around the frustration and redirection of the powerful diencephalic drives related to sex.

While it is generally agreed that a healthy sex life can be important to the well-ordered life of an individual, there is little guarantee that powerful impulses may not break in on the best ordered life to take over behavior and produce personal and social crises. This may occur at times when there are contributive factors such as rapid modification of glandular function, as occurs in adolescence and involution. Or it may be released by nonrational impulses set in motion by contiguity to a powerfully stimulating sex object. Whatever the circumstantial cause, they may disorganize normal behavior, create crises of family and community life, and release guilt and remorse on one side and hostility and jealousy on the other.

Other crises may develop with threats to the individual's security system. The person who is well organized and good humored may show major personality changes when he loses his employment and is faced with economic and social insecurity. He may become hostile and strike out at persons for no apparent reason. When his sources of inner safety are disrupted, he may be so threatened that he will take what appear to be unreasonable defensive or unreasonably self-destructive forms of behavior. If the stress is great enough, he may even murder others or commit suicide. The behavior is observed by others as nonrational, but within the individual it is a response that was not lifted to the level of rational action because the diencephalic forces were so strong they produced the actions before becoming subject to the normal rational controls of the individual.

When people respond to these basic forces set in motion by primitive anatomical equipment, they not only are mystified by what they have done but, after the more rational perspective is restored, tend to be highly judgmental of themselves. The burden of guilt and remorse adds to the problems that already exist. The civilized man begins to contemplate the apparent savage hidden at the core of his being.

If we are to understand and wisely manage the crises that

emerge in life, it is important for us to see some of the mechanisms underlying our behavior. For the very behavior that is a primitive response to crises at one level of human experience may be the cause of other and more significant crises.

6

The Physiology of Crisis

We have looked at the inner mechanisms of primitive origins that respond to crises in our environment and may even create them in our spontaneous behavior. Now we will explore in greater depth some aspects of our behavior in crises.

Some of this behavior is organic or physiological. Research in psychosomatic medicine works on the assumption that all behavior has meaning. Illness as a form of organic behavior has its own special type of meaning. If we can discover the meaning in this organic behavior, we have moved a step closer to the possibility of controlling the illness.

A personality crisis may set in motion inner and conflicting emotions that use the body as their battleground. The term disease probably well describes the state of being that exists, for the being is not at ease with itself and the diseased state of being is acted out by the disease system or the organic structure that is most responsive to the inner disturbance.

It has been observed that the weakest link in the organic system tends to be most responsive to the inner conflict and so first shows the symptoms that indicate the battle raging within an individual. If a person has a strong physical structure, the breakdown or disease may show itself in emotional problems. If the person has great strength at the psychic level and can manage his emotional behavior, it may well show up in the physical system where some weakness may exist.

Let us illustrate the way various physical systems can engage themselves in acting out inner emotional states. When John experienced severe business reverses, he began to drink heavily. When he was at home, he was difficult to manage. When he was away from home, his wife Emma was constantly worried that he would be arrested for driving under the influence of alcohol, or have an accident where he or someone else might be killed or seriously injured. As time went on and Emma seemed helpless in trying to control the situation, she became more irritated and frustrated.

Emma began to have itchy skin. She went to a dermatologist, who diagnosed it as psoriasis. Tests were made for allergies, but no treatment seemed to help. Emma's skin condition progressed until she was not able to wear stockings or anything on her arms. When the condition covered her arms and legs and began to show itself on her back and abdomen, she was almost beside herself with the constant irritation and itching. Salves helped the immediate skin condition but did not stop it from spreading to other parts of the body. After six months of the finest medical care available the condition was worse.

John was arrested after a minor accident and the judge suggested that he join Alcoholics Anonymous. There he found a fellowship and an outlet for his compulsive behavior. He determined to control his drinking by accepting and giving help. As soon as he stopped drinking, Emma's psoriasis began to disappear and within two months there was no trace of it.

It is not difficult to see the relationship between Emma's massive irritation at her husband and the response of the skin, the organ of sensation for the body. The best medical care was not able to reduce the organic acting out of the irritation. But when the cause of the irritation disappeared, so also the organic evidence of the irritation ceased to exist. John's crisis was transferred to Emma, who acted it out in her body. When John's resolution of his crisis took place, Emma was freed of the irritation and her body no longer was involved in acting out its distress in physical symptoms.

Other body systems can become involved in this organic behavior of acting out emotional stress. Sometimes the cause-effect factors may be so apparently unrelated that it is difficult to see the connection between body symptom and emotional state.

While serving as professor of psychiatry at Harvard Medical School, Erich Lindemann did research on ulcerative colitis. There seemed to be emotional factors related to the disease but they were obscure, so detailed personal histories were taken of a large number of persons suffering from this distressing and hard-to-treat malady.

When the research findings were correlated, it seemed scientifically and statistically significant that over eighty percent of the persons studied had had an acute grief experience in the six-month period preceding the onset of the symptoms. It also seemed that the patients had had difficulty in managing the crises created by their grief.

At first it would seem rather far-fetched to assume that the inner conflict related to unwisely managed grief would show up in anything as apparently separated from the emotions as the colon. It was decided to explore the dynamics of grief to understand what the connection might be.

The important task of the process of mourning is to let go of the lost love object so that the invested emotion can be retrieved and the mourner can become a whole person able to reinvest his love where it can enrich and sustain life. But the person who could not do the work of mourning wisely began to repress his feelings. The feelings continued to exist and found alternate routes for expressing themselves.

The body began to symbolically express its inability to let go. It held onto body waste until it fermented, giving rise to the development of acids and other substances that caused irritation of the surrounding tissue of the large intestine. This irritation eventually led to inflammation of the tissue, and this in time caused tissue breakdown with the incident ulceration. So the body with its own processes entered into the emotional crisis and tried to act out the feelings that were not managed openly and honestly.

Other forms of involvement of the alimentary canal may not be as obscure as ulcerative colitis. Forms of aggression may show up in diseases of the teeth. Anxiety may manifest itself in globus hystericus where the mechanisms of swallowing tend to misfunction. Anxiety may produce stomach ulcers, and other forms of fear may show up in everything from a dry mouth to butterflies in the stomach or loss of sphincter control.

The heart has been a symbol for the emotions from early times. Men felt their hearts pound in the presence of emotional stimuli. The common language describes the varied ways the heart reacted: My heart jumped, my heart was in my throat, my heart stopped still, my heart tells me, my heart is full.

Mrs. B. was a sensitive and quite vulnerable woman. She was self-centered and critical of others. When her husband had what was called a nervous breakdown, she was determined that he not become involved in psychotherapy because she felt it might reveal things about her that she did not want shared with anyone, no matter what her husband's health needs might be.

She told her husband that if he went to a psychiatrist she would kill him, probably more an expression of her disturbance than a clear expression of intent. When she found that her husband had been referred to a psychotherapist, she called to assure the counselor that if he continued to see her husband she would kill him also. Again this was probably hyperbole.

Two months later her husband died of a heart attack, and within a month Mrs. B., who had never shown indications of any physical difficulties with her heart, died of a similar form of heart attack. The identification with her husband combined with her deep anxiety about her own behavior apparently brought about the organic malfunction that was life-destroying.

One study of widows shows that the death rate among widows during the year following the death of a husband is 700 percent higher than that of other women the same age. The emotional crisis is dramatically acted out physiologically in the organic malfunction implicit in these statistics.

The glandular system is most immediately responsive to emotional stimulus. The defense systems of the body are closely related to glandular function. If you hear a sad story, you may stimulate the lacrymal glands and begin to weep. If you see a juicy steak, you may begin to salivate even though you are not hungry. If you experience a sexual stimulation, another set of glands may immediately go to work.

The glandular system is the chemical factory of the body, providing a variety of chemicals to give muscle tone and added strength when threatened, chemicals to facilitate digestion when eating, and chemicals to maintain homeostasis within the body to meet the varied conditions of atmospheric and environmental stress the body encounters.

However, there are times when the stresses of life become so acute that they overtax the glandular system's ability to meet these needs. This may be true especially when the environment changes so rapidly that the primitive equipment of the body no longer seems pertinent to the body's needs. When the adrenal glands flood the body with the chemicals that make it possible to fight or flee from danger, the system may be oversupplied with chemicals it cannot use.

Malfunction of the glandular system in relation to the needs of modern man produces the organic acting out that is called disease. E. Weaver Johnson, in her study of diabetes, says that it appeared that the chronic demand upon the glands for sugar to meet the internal energy crisis overtaxed the pancreas. W. C. Menninger comments on the remarkable coincidences of emotional shock and the onset of diabetes.

Even in the more obscure etiological factors of cancer it appears that glandular malfunction may be at work to produce the conditions that favor the development of neoplastic tissue. Lawrence LeShan, in his study of spontaneous regressions in malignancies, found that in deep explorations of the conscious and unconscious mental life of the cancer patient there appeared to be a correlation between the onset of the disease and the emotional crisis that the patient experienced prior to the first symptoms. As LeShan explains it, the poorly managed crisis produced a chronic imbalance in body chemistry. With the probability of abnormal cell division hundreds of times a day, the body is dependent upon the normal body chemistry to control the abnormal cell division. But when there is a chronic imbalance, the control mechanisms are so disturbed that the abnormal cell division may run rampant and show up as the neoplastic tissue that tears other organ systems apart. LeShan points out that in his studies there has almost invariably been a major emotional trauma in the life of the cancer patient, and that sometimes the treatment of the unresolved emotional crisis apparently produced so significant a change in body chemistry that a spontaneous regression appeared under the most carefully observed hospital conditions.

The muscle system is clearly involved in the acting out of emotional crises. Expressions of the face, from a look of horror to contorted features in various forms of excitement, are commonly observed, as is the clenching of a fist, in anger. Internal tension may show in the conflicts of muscle systems that produce tremor. Chronic breakdown of muscle function observed in arthritis and similar diseases may be related to chronic emotional crises. But the idioms of common language show an awareness of the close relation of emotional states to musculature: He squared his shoulders, he kept a stiff upper lip, he held his head high, he was on his toes at once, he went limp, he had no backbone, he was hamstrung, he froze in his tracks. It is also indicated that the effect of emotional stress may be observed in the involuntary muscle systems, and that the ancient needs for rest and relaxation are clearly related to the need for a cessation of the muscle tensions that produce organic conflicts.

What is true for other major body systems is also observed in the relation of emotional crises to the way our sensory equipment functions. Again, common language gives us some clues: He turned up his nose, he's hearing things, his eyes almost popped out of his head. If we think of kinesthesis and inner balance as extensions of sensory awareness, the language is equally explicit: He felt uplifted or he suffered a terrific letdown, he has lost his balance or he is badly shaken.

Witnesses under emotional stress are often discredited in court for their inability to separate emotional stimuli from accurate sensory awareness. The state of mind or emotion may well sharpen perception in one area at the same time that it is dulling it in another. So people are urged not to make decisions with long-term consequences when they are caught off balance by emotional crises.

It becomes quite clear that emotional crises may affect all the major physiological systems of the body. When the crisis is worked out through immediate response, the system tends to return to normal rather quickly. But when the emotional state becomes chronic through a person's inability to work through the crisis, the functioning of the whole system may be so disrupted that disease control systems may break down and infections run rampant, viral formations take new life, and cell division get out of control.

To understand the impact of crises upon our lives physiologically, it is always important to be objective about our own behavior and the behavior of others so that we interpret the organic functions we observe in terms of the unusual stress. A person who is rendered unconscious by a blow on the head or a person in a coma is responding to stress through the specialized organic behavior that blots out consciousness. In milder form, stress and crises may reduce awareness and limit the capacity for response. The need for understanding the physical basis for the observed behavior may be more difficult with the limited or modified conditions that often occur when a person seems not to be himself, but the need for interpreting the behavior wisely may be even more important than when it is clearly obvious.

In times of acute crises it is usually safe and wise to be extra kind to yourself and others. Our physical equipment is complicated and mystifying. We need to give ourselves and others the advantage of the doubt until all the facts are in and the basis for organic behavior is more clearly understood. Our anatomical endowment and our physical functioning may respond to crises in ways that demand all our skill in careful perception and wise interpretation of what is happening to people under unusual stress.

7

The Anthropology of Crisis

Crises happen to people but they always happen to people in context. The context of a crisis can be sociological or anthropological or both. For our purposes we will try to separate the contexts in the next two chapters, although we know that in life it cannot easily be done.

Anthropology is the study of man, the things he does, the things he feels, and the social patterns that emerge from his thinking, acting, and feeling. Some studies of man go into his earlier development and produce what we refer to as primitive anthropology. Other studies look at man in the context of his living now and constitute cultural anthropology. Both types of study throw light on the way man has dealt with the crises of his personal life.

Studies of man, the animal, look back at the points where his roots in animal existence determined his behavior. Evolutionary factors were clearly at work to determine some of the capacities for relationship and feeling that lie at the roots of our concepts of personal crises.

Somewhere back in the distant past, the more highly developed anthropoids went through major changes in their life patterns. These changes produced racial memory set deep in levels of consciousness. This means that certain types of behavior are caused not so much by present relations as by the impact of the past. For instance, Eskimos' guilt dreams are often centered on snakes although there are no serpents in regions where Eskimos now live. The fear that some people have of mice is not determined by the threat that these small creatures now have for humans—the apprehension appears to be rooted in the intrusion of creatures into the caves where cavemen dwelt through long hours of darkness with no way of knowing what was crawling over them.

The animal or the primitive adapted and adjusted to his environment over long periods of time, and some of the modifications have been so deeply grooved in consciousness that they continue to assert themselves with power even now through physiological and neural patterns of behavior.

The basic animal needs are practical ones, such as rest, food, sex, shelter, flight, and fight. Many of our contemporary crises are related to these areas of experience. If rest patterns are disturbed and a person cannot sleep, he may become ill or disturbed. Preoccupation with eating and dieting is a central focus for many people, and the disturbances of eating cause much personal distress. Sex and conflicts between lifestyles are the point where primitive and contemporary sex needs are brought into critical focus. The problems of architecture are built around the needs for shelter; energy crises related to heat and light are the distant echo of the caveman's dilemmas. The desire for a second home in the mountains or by the sea is an expression of concern about flight from the stress and pressure that disrupt life. The defense budgets and military establishments that draw off the major economic strength of many countries are the more destructive expressions of the ancient concern for self-preservation.

Under stress there appears to be a retreat to the more primitive forms of problem-solving. One philosopher has even projected what he calls a biogenetic law, which implies that each individual in his development recapitulates all of the past history of the process of human development.

Eilhard Von Domaris says it is important to relate psychiatry and anthropology because it is impossible to understand the behavior of modern man without exploring the sources of that behavior. He claims that early in anthropoid development some ancestors of the apes took to the trees, and so solved many of their problems of survival. While their relatives on the ground had to be ferocious to stay alive, the tree apes had plenty of fruit for food, protection in their secluded habitat, and the kind of leisure and security that made it possible for them to develop long-term interest in other members of their group. So mating began to take on social meaning instead of being merely an instinctive compulsion. Parents began to show extended interest in their offspring. So the mental and emotional development of the tree apes produced the capacity for relationships that emerged into loving concern. When the apes were able to invest this concern in others, they could suffer loss and know grief and emotional crises.

With the potential for this deep feeling emerging from the accidents of the evolutionary process, man was in a position to develop it further. When man was a nomadic hunter with little social structure or home life, he functioned largely on the basis of a simple form of self-awareness. But the emergence of agriculture brought stability into human relationships and hastened the growth of a group consciousness that could express itself in superego qualities, conscience, and primitive legal structures. With the development of cities for protection and industrialization, the concern with an ever-increasing fabric of interrelationships produced both new securities and new stresses. Von Domaris says that the only solution for the problems man has created by his rapidly developing social structures is to develop a new concept of cosmic man, with an appreciation of the sacredness of all life. This religious man must develop a new set of standards for shared life on the earth. We may be seeing some movement in that direction with ecumenical religions, ecological concern for the shared environment, and international organizations coping with common problems of food, health, security, and life resources.

The deep-rooted emotional drives incident to these basic patterns inherited from the distant past are reflected in the behavior of the old savage in the new civilization. Let us look at some of these types of behavior, for they are related to many of the personal crises we experience day after day.

Actually the concept of sanity is related to our security system for we feel comfortable with the known, which we call the normal. We feel uncomfortable with the unknown or the deviant. If someone told us that a cow had five legs, we would be apt to say he was crazy for all the cows we have ever seen had four legs. But perhaps in a circus sideshow he did see a five-legged cow, and he acted on his unusual experience. Deviant perception or abnormal behavior so challenges our known frame of reference that we cannot tolerate it and so we try to exclude those who threaten us. So the five-legged cows are outlawed along with those who say they have seen them.

When people are so insecure in their human relations that they are unable to function, they tend to revert to earlier ways of behaving. The neurotic adult can act like a child and throw a tantrum. The threatened social group can also revert to earlier defensive forms of behavior, and employ emotion in the place of reason as its problem-solving method. This is why truth is always the first casualty in warfare. Truth summons reason, while the emotions necessary for armed conflict must depend on something more primitive.

Overeating also is related to primitive needs that continue to motivate behavior long after the original conditions are gone. When our ancestors killed a deer, they would gorge themselves in a meal that might not be repeated for days. The system was defending itself against starvation by storing as much energy for life as possible. Some people are still motivated to eat more than is necessary even though there is a promise of three square meals every day. The main method of those who set up diet control groups is to establish a new compulsion about not eating that is strong enough to combat the deeply rooted compulsion to eat all you can whenever you can just because it is there. Although the methods of agricultural societies have been around for 5,000 years, the anthropological compulsions from deep within have not caught up with new ways of handling nourishment for our bodies.

Also rooted in our natures as emerging evolutionary creatures is what we call animus. This is clearly related to what we generally think of as animal behavior. Some aspects of animal behavior carry so much hostility that another word we often use to describe it is animosity. The deeply planted root of our security expresses itself in a need to protect our nests and employ pugnacity to that end. The lowly stickleback is a little fish that is as vicious as a barracuda near its nest but becomes increasingly docile as it gets farther away from home. A wildcat is seldom seen because of its timid habits of retreat from other creatures, especially man. But if cornered near its habitat, it can fight with the ferocity that leads us to speak of "fighting like a wildcat."

The defense of property has primitive roots. Many societies have evolved to the point where property is valued primarily for its use and not just for its possession. Indians on the North American continent were often misunderstood, for they felt everyone had a right to use what he needed and must share with others as their need warranted. When Europeans started colonization, Indians often shared with them according to their need and felt free to take back what they had shared when they needed it. This led to the term "Indian giver" and caused much conflict.

In terms of tribal perspectives the motivations of capitalism, with the high status given to the ownership of private property, are more closely related to the primitive security systems than to the advanced ideas of shared use according to need. Much conflict in recent years both personally and nationally has been related to concepts of sacred rights of possession rather than shared rights to natural resources.

Some ecological problems we face are bound up with the implicit rights of exploitation that go with absolute ownership. If the earth belongs to an individual, he can do anything he chooses with it no matter what it does to the future possibility for use of the land. Mining, especially strip mining, has illustrated this concept of exploitation.

The changes sought by those in favor of women's liberation are also bound up with property rights. Many ancient legal systems assumed that a woman was her husband's property. Laws concerning adultery were based on the fact that no one had a right to use a man's sexual property, and in some cultures the crime was so serious that the death penalty was exacted. A woman's rights to her own being were overshadowed by the concept of private property, and only now is the whole concept being subjected to major examination and reform.

Other aspects of human sexuality are related to deep roots from the past. In the evolutionary process reproduction was unisexual for long eras of time. Bisexuality was a rather late development fraught with problems. The sex act was empowered by nature with such aggressive force that frogs had horns to hold the female and other reptiles had hooks. Chickens in the barnyard engage in sexual activity with the clear impression of aggression. Even though social patterns have modified the expressions of sexuality among humans, the male is usually considered the wolf and the female the peacock. And forced sexuality, the act of rape, is often dealt with as if it were a major criminal act. So many aspects of contemporary behavior have their roots deep in anthropological processes well behind us in time.

Two natures appear to be constantly at work in man—his amity and his enmity. His social structure depends on trust and indications of friendliness. Yet implicit in much of his behavior is suspicion, distrust, and wariness. Both forces exist and must be understood. Darwin elaborated on the descent of man as a part of nature, "red in tooth and claw." With this picture of man we have been inclined to glorify competition as if it were man's major endowment. But Kropotkin wrote just as convincingly about the mutual aid factor in evolution. In nature and in anthropology there has long been a strong impulse to find strength and security in the development of cooperation and goodwill. Many religious traditions have been built on this impulse toward cooperation, and some major economic and social patterns have employed this concept.

However, some of the directions we see operative in contemporary culture seem to be reversions. In our highly scientific and technologically advanced culture it seems that there has been a loss of moral responsibility, yet in a complex culture man needs morality to govern the power he can produce. The struggle between the two natures in man creates many crises, but the understanding of the roots of the conflict may help resolve them.

Originally man needed to use all the power he could develop just to survive. So he increased the power of his strong right arm with a club and projected his power with the thrown spear. But there came a time when he had a surplus of power. He had more power available than he needed to survive. So he tended to adapt this power to survive into power to control. The scientist usually has had objectives other than morality, so most scientists have been more amoral than moral. The major impact of their research and inventiveness went to increase power for the control of nature and other men without concern about the niceties of moral behavior or ethical structures. Other forces in society worked for the control of the power. Such forms as dictatorships enhanced the power of government, and more democratic traditions tended to protect individuals from the abuse of power. But in governments where scientists have had commanding influence, moral and ethical lag has been observed.

But even in social groups seeking to extend moral controls, there have been anthropological throwbacks binding the past into the present. Taboos against cannibalism and incest have been powerful and deep-rooted. Some theories on migraine headaches suggest that they manifest organic revulsion against eating flesh that sends massive amounts of blood to constrict blood vessels in the brain, producing the pain of congestion. Religious institutions have tried to meet this threat by establishing ceremonial meals that symbolically deal with the taboos of cannibalism in emotionally sterilized surroundings. It is sufficient for our purpose here to point out that we have not separated ourselves from the early problems but have built them into our development so that we are still contending with them.

This is also true of the taboo against incest. Racial experience showed that incest was hazardous. There were no legal and social structures to restrain such behavior, so by a long and slow process the taboo was built into the anthropological restraints on the race. Instead of relating to family members, the sexual objects most closely accessible, the taboo made them sexually threatening. A different mood and climate bound those who were close. When people wanted to extend this area of close relationship, they built other groups who shared the taboos and added to the self-imposed restraints. So fraternities and secret societies developed and enhanced the mood of the incest taboos. Many secret societies have the stipulation that there can be no sexual activity with spouses of the group members under threat of rigorous punishment such as death or castration. This incest taboo can also be projected into various forms of social and racial prejudice. Many of the more acute forms of personal and social crises that we experience cannot be easily separated from these deeply stored emotional protections that have long been employed by social groups.

The conflicts between the ingroups and the outgroups are still at work. Interracial and interreligious marriages often stir up deep emotional responses out of all proportion to the human problems explicit in the relationships. Here we see manifestations of the impact of primitive and cultural anthropology at work.

We cannot cope with the crises that impinge on our personal and social experience without recognizing that, more than we may ever realize, we are confronting ancient problems and long-used problem-solving techniques in a context that should have outgrown both the problems and the inadequate methods for solving them.

8

The Sociology of Crisis

With the exception of an occasional hermit, people live together in groups. Their lives are structured by the life of the group. The folkways, the adequacy of language, the modes of communication and relationship are the very stuff of which an individual's life is made. And the individuals in a group are always at work to confirm, modify, or challenge the group's lifestyle. When change is almost nonexistent, we have a conservative or static form of social life. When change is rapid, we observe radical or revolutionary change. When change is constant but controlled, we speak of the evolutionary process at work.

The social structure within which a person works can make him sick or contribute to his health. People respond differently to social processes. Most people thrown into the distorted lifestyle of a prison tend to become increasingly sick, but there are rare instances of a John Bunyan or a George Fox who turned the prison experience into something creative. For the thousands who died of the social sickness promoted in German concentration camps, there were some, psychoanalyst Viktor Frankl for example, who used the tragic circumstances productively.

When a society is alive with great self-confidence, it stimulates creativity. One thinks immediately of the Age of Pericles, the Renaissance, and Elizabethan England as times when men believed in themselves and produced the creative fruits of their self-awareness.

Sociology is the study of the ways people live and work together. As most of the crises of life are related to the people who influence our lives, it is quite clear that the impact of a healthy or sick society will have great bearing on the skills people develop for managing crises.

Social patterns have a life of their own, and what may be healthy at one time may become maladaptive when circumstances change. We see this illustrated now in the crisis of the city. Originally people came to cities for protection and security, both from wild animals that roamed in profusion and from enemies who might be less apt to attack a city. Then cities became cultural centers and people lived in them because of the advantages they provided with universities, museums, concerts, and other cultural benefits that were not so easily found in small villages or the open countryside.

But the city that once brought benefits of security and culture now provides quite the opposite. Taxes have increased so that it is economically disadvantageous to live in the city. The prevalence of crime makes it difficult for people to take advantage of the cultural life because they are afraid to go out at night. Within the lifetime of many of us, the city has changed from a healthy to a sick environment and people's lives have been modified by the change. Many of the crises of air pollution, crime, economic strangulation, and social blight are evidence of the social change in our cities from sources of health to sources of illness.

Similarly the escapes people employ to get beyond the threats of the cities may be equally damaging. Some people seek relief from tension through increased use of chemical desensitization or popular forms of drug addiction. The use of hard drugs to get beyond the stress of ghetto living has produced much of the crime that in turn makes the environment more critical.

Other people try to escape the city by getting out into the

country, so urban sprawl reaches farther out into the country. This creates travel problems that increase traffic on the highways, expand the network of expressways cutting through the countryside, and fill the air we breathe with ever-increasing amounts of noxious gases. Then many of the same problems that have plagued the cities are transferred to the suburbs, and drugs, crime, and other forms of blight follow. The increased energy drain uses up the limited source of fuel supplies so that insecurity spreads and anxiety grows. Thus efforts to escape from stress in turn create more stress and the sickness spreads with the crises incident to it.

What has happened to cities has also happened to whole countries. Studies of contemporary England show how basic values have changed in fifty years. Before World War I England had a measure of security about the world that gave self-confidence to Englishmen whatever their station in life. They felt proud to be what they were. Then the war came with its frightful losses and there was hardly an English family that was not affected by the devastation. While some of the pride remained, there was economic difficulty, social readjustment, and a loss of confidence.

When World War II came there was less enthusiasm for an international mission. The period between the wars had not produced a consolidation of values, and the rumblings about collapse of empire shattered confidence. While there was a deep commitment that could be directed toward heroic and sacrificial action, morale was tinctured more with despair than with great hope. When there was a rapid falling apart of empire following 1945, the English character suffered. Just as his society became increasingly withdrawn and deeply wounded, so the individual Englishman took on more of the characteristics of the sociopath, became less apt to act from conviction and more interested in himself, more concerned with manipulating others and less interested in identification with others, and his social and moral standards in relation to the rest of society suffered. Less inspired by the past and less hopeful about the future, the society and its members became increasingly sick, and this illness showed itself in many facets of life.

Similar trends have been observed in American life. As society, politics, and industry have become more impersonal, dehumanized, and depersonalized, men have pulled life in about themselves. There was less interest in the past or future and more concern for satisfying immediate impulses and appetites. This has been damaging to our sense of tradition which is rooted in the past, as well as to our ethical concerns which are determined by present action with future consequences. Life became more and more materialistic, personal success was measured in materialistic ways, and the quest for pleasure took the place of the experience of happiness.

So we see evidences of sick behavior all about us with high government officials praising a mental defective who murders in cold blood dozens of defenseless women and children at the same time that the same governmental officials are spending millions of public dollars to try to discredit scholars and priests whose only crime has been to oppose brutality and seek to make the truth accessible to the community at large. No one living in a larger community that shows such corrosion of moral standards can help but be involved with the sickness in one way or another.

The conflict of sick and healthy forces in society has persisted over long periods of time. Where great power was in jeopardy, powerful action was taken against those who challenged the status quo.

Such was the case with the Cathars or Cathari in medieval times. Concerned by the power of the church and its influence over people's lives, priests and laymen tried to move back toward the original and purer impulse of the church's origin. Employing less dramatic services, they dedicated themselves to the practice of loving concern for their neighbors and strong opposition to war and abusive power in any form. Strongly influenced by St. Francis, the Cathari created communities where shared resources improved economic life. They tried to make the world beautiful and they were derisively referred to as the flower children.

But the Cathari created problems. The improved conditions of life in the cities where they lived threatened the feudal system. People were not inclined to endure slavery in a feudal manor when they could have freedom among the Cathari. The church, with its dependence on the economic power of feudalism, was distressed by the rapid growth in numbers and influence of the Cathari. So people were sent into the Franciscan organization to disrupt it and a special crusade was organized among feudal princes. One of the bloodiest of history, it brought the murders of tens of thousands of men, women, and children who refused to fight or defend themselves. Some small remnants retreated into the hills of northern Italy and still maintain their small Albigensian and Anabaptist communities there.

The conflict between the entrenched power of the church as an institution and the freedom-loving Cathari has been recapitulated again and again in history where the sick and healthy parts of society cannot abide side by side. These conflicts have not ceased.

Social purpose large enough to sustain major values seems to produce healthy social life. The cities along the coast of England maintained excellent morale as long as they were under fire from enemy guns across the Channel. The quality of health and the structure of community life were maintained at a high level. But as soon as the assault ended, bickering set in and morale collapsed—with a related breakdown of personal health.

Viktor Frankl, in his book *From Death Camp to Existentialism,* says that as long as people in the German prison camps were able to keep up hope and look to the future with some feeling that their torture would cease, they were able to survive. When their sense of purpose was gone, something inside of them caved in—their will to survive faded—and they were soon dead.

Joost Meerloo's studies of panic point out that as long as people can be kept busy helping others and doing something that is constructive, panic does not grip them. When the crisis is past they are apt to panic, actually when there is no longer good reason. We observe in personal experience that in a critical moment we may perform with courage and wisdom, only to begin to shake and fall apart after the crisis is over. The motivation of worthy purpose is a part of the healthy social structure.

The social patterns that are an important part of a child's education can be healthy or unhealthy. The child who is brought up on a farm with important tasks to do and responsibility for machinery and property is less apt to engage in vandalism than those who have no comparable direction for their energy. A boy raised in a congested area, with no constructive outlet for his energy, is more apt to find ways for expressing his energy that destroy people and property.

The child who lives in a world of constant violence can become calloused to behavior that injures others. A survey of television programming points out that the average child who watches television during the children's hours sees and hears over 13,000 acts of violence, assault, murder, and armed robbery during the ages of three to thirteen. This may well be the projection of a sick image into the informal education of children.

The social resources that can help people wisely cope with their personal crises have to do with purpose, education, and social values. But there is another factor of importance. When life is surrounded by love, people feel secure. When love fails, life shows the effect.

When military personnel landed on Okinawa and the usual inoculation of civilians took place, it was observed that the children seemed to have no apprehension. They put up their arms for the injections with no indication that they thought they might feel pain. Further observation showed that there were virtually no neurotics or psychotics, even after one of the most merciless bombings in human history. The psychologists brought in to explore the meaning of this discovery checked into social patterns, child training methods, and general health.

Some of their conclusions reflect a healthy and loving society. Children are treated with constant love and concern. From the time of birth children are strapped to their parents' backs and are constantly the focus of attention and conversation. Children are not punished until they are old enough to understand the meaning of misbehavior, and punishment is seldom necessary since the children develop concern for others just as they have been the center of concern.

Children in Okinawa do not expect adults to deliberately injure a child, so they are not likely to fear a doctor. The children are so secure in the atmosphere of love that they grow to value themselves and so are able to value others. Because they have built into the core of their being a basic trust of others, they are fortified against stress, and even constant bombing did not appear to disrupt this inner state of being.

A society that reflects love to a child early in life is one that makes it possible for a child to be loving. The child who is denied love and given abuse instead may find it difficult to love and may even become a sociopath.

The basic social forces that influence the development of personality start with the family. School also has an important role to play. Political structures can create social modes of trust or distrust. Feelings are more important than intellectualizations in the child's growth. Play is important experimental living. Attitudes toward sex may have long-lasting impact on life. If attitudes toward sex are restrictive, the feeling component of sex life may be permanently inhibited. If love can be expressed freely, sex may become a legitimate part of this loving attitude in life. Religious attitudes also have a bearing on the perspectives of life, and healthy or sick religion produces its appropriate response in personality development. The problem areas of life are never far separated from the social structure that frames the developing personality.

Social attitudes may breed class wars, may produce the conditions of illness with the accompanying effect of absenteeism. Society can create the conditions of unemployment and economic conflict through strikes. It can produce the conditions that lead to migrations and the breaking of ties with old and established ways of doing things. With all these social conditions come personal dislocations that become the crises people must cope with.

Social fragmentation may produce personal instability as the individual is separated from social patterns that provide established and comfortable ways of doing things. When one family in five moves every year, it can be seen that old family and community patterns may be disrupted. This can fracture relationships and communication when they are most essential. When teenagers from different backgrounds move into houses next door to each other, the conflict of patterns may begin to cause stress. One girl may be encouraged to start dating at age twelve while the other family may have a strict view that no dating is acceptable until the age of eighteen. In no time at all the conflict of social patterns may cause alienation between children and parents, and generalized confusion over the right and wrong way to live.

Often the social patterns that are at work to produce the crises and conflicts of life are unexamined and inherited. If we are going to learn to manage the crises of life wisely, it is important for us to develop skills in examining social patterns, evaluating differing moral and social codes, and discovering what is valid and useful for us at the time and place in which we live.

9

The Psychology of Crisis

Psychology is the study of human behavior with a primary concern for understanding its meaning. It is a psychological maxim that all behavior is meaningful even though sometimes the meaning may be nonrational and obscure. That merely means one must look more patiently and persistently for the meaning.

The psychology of crisis is the study of people in times of crisis to see how they behave and then to understand what the behavior means. When this principle was applied to the study of illness as a form of organic behavior, a whole new stage of medical advancement began to take place. Questions were asked about psychosomatic and psychogenic ailments that had not been asked before. (*Psychosomatic* ailments involve the interrelation of mind and body; *psychogenic* disease originates in the emotions. All disease, then, is psychosomatic, but only some is psychogenic.) Physicians inquired as to the meaning of the symptoms they observed. When they asked the right questions, they began to get a whole new set of answers.

However, illness is but one of the areas of human behavior now being explored in search of elusive but significant meanings. Research in crisis psychology has made great advances in the past decade, and we are now beginning to share its benefits.

In later chapters we will look at some of the precise findings about the crises at various stages of personality development. Here we will make an initial examination of the insights gained from crisis psychology to see what it is and how it works.

Life is a process. The energy of life directs people toward goals and forms of fulfillment. When progress toward these goals is frustrated, various forms of behavior may be observed. Sometimes the person capitulates to circumstance: He becomes a defeated individual who gives up and ceases to use his energy toward his goals.

Three major classifications of psychological behavior define types of response to life circumstances: character disorder, neurotic behavior, and psychotic behavior. Character disorders usually have their roots early in life. Normal development in communication and relationship is thwarted, and the child retreats into the lonely regions of his inner being. Because his capacity for normal feelings has not fully developed, he is not usually able to be aware of the feelings of others. So he tends to manipulate and use others rather than to have emotional responses to them.

This type of character disorder not only is a response to personal crisis early in life but also tends to produce crises in the lives of others. Many criminals, especially "con men" and those who manipulate others, act out their character limitations as if they were minus a conscience. People who marry spouses with character disorders are apt to suffer endlessly, for a normal person expects normal responses from one who is apparently incapable of it.

A second type of response to crisis is the neurotic form of behavior. The person who suffers from a neurosis feels excessive anxiety much of the time. When he cannot cope with the anxiety in usual forms of action, he retreats into earlier types of problem-solving. Usually this makes his problem worse, for the earlier forms of behavior are inappropriate. A tantrum by a three-year-old might be tolerated because of age, but a tantrum by a thirty-three-year-old is far less acceptable and usually creates crises. So it is with the obsessive-compulsive person, who tends to overdo everything from his drinking to his symptoms of illness. He may even turn his anxieties into paralyzing physical symptoms as escapes from stress. Soldiers who become temporarily blind in battle are in effect saying, "Stop the shooting. Can't you see I'm helpless?"

The neurotic response to crisis usually projects the problems out upon those who share the home, the office, or the school. The neurotic person tends to spread his conflicts and make others irritable, suspicious, and disturbed. He sets people against people as though increased crisis around him in the lives of others could reduce his own stress. It is usually difficult for people who are meeting their stresses within normal bounds to tolerate the excesses of the neurotic. Neuroses can be quite uncomfortable for the neurotic person and those around him, for they distort human relations and create more problems. But they can be treated, and this eases the pain and stress.

The third type of response to stress is psychotic. Here the stress is so great that the person cannot cope with it in the normal process of living. While the neurotic may continue to work—while making himself and others miserable—the psychotic tends to lose touch with reality and may become nonfunctional. He may become so suspicious that he does not dare eat because he thinks his food may be poisoned. He may find the real world so intolerable that he will retreat into an unreal world where he feels more comfortable, but it is a world that is out of context with others and produces a hazardous nonconformity that is apt to be life-disrupting.

While the neurotic person knows something is wrong, the psychotic may have severe thought disturbances. He may think he is the only one who sees things as they are and everyone else is disturbed. The emotional life of the psychotic may be observed in extremes. There may be little or no emotional response to pain or acute crises on one hand or extremes of rage and shouting on the other. The psychotic may be so absorbed in his unreal inner world that he becomes incapable of caring for himself and needs custodial care to maintain physical functioning. Improved methods of care make it possible to treat many psychotics so that they can return to more normal living.

Within the more usual range the meaning of crises from the psychological point of view is related to the adequacy of the person in coping with stress. Two types of stressful circumstances may be observed. One has to do with a crisis that can be seen well in advance, and the other is the crisis that occurs abruptly and without a chance for preparation.

When in school we prepared for examinations. At the beginning of the term we knew that within a certain number of weeks we would face a time of testing. We could carefully prepare each day as the term proceeded, or we could wait for a cram session at the end. Either way, we were able to decide in advance how we would cope with a crisis we knew was coming.

But the crises that usually cause the most trouble are the ones that pounce on us without warning. All may be going well until suddenly an accident happens to us or to someone important to us. Then in an instant everything is disrupted; we are uncertain and confused. We have to draw on resources that have been built up in periods of personality development to meet the immediate and threatening circumstance.

Here the impact of frustration and conflict must be confronted with nothing but what we have developed within ourselves. How do we learn to meet frustration? How do we learn to manage conflicts?

What is it that usually causes frustration? Almost always, our frustration emerges where an impulse to act is blocked. Sometimes this is done by environmental conditions: It may rain when we want to play golf or tennis. At other times it may be an external circumstance we cannot control: We may be in a hurry to get somewhere and find we have to make a long and dusty detour.

Some of the more difficult forms of frustration are related to our own limitations or feelings of inadequacy. We want to win in an intercollegiate track meet, but we just cannot make our legs move fast enough. We want to get a good position, but on the day of the interview we are so nervous that we make a poor impression. We want to win an audition and are so filled with stage fright that we become choked up and function well below our potential. So we become furious with ourselves, for we are the cause of our own frustration.

Sometimes we are not able to function adequately because of inner conflict. We have a job to do but cannot seem to do it because we really want to be somewhere else and doing something else. We were called into the shop for some overtime work on the very evening we had tickets for a play our daughter was in; and, because our motivations were in conflict, the evening dragged on with no end of irritations and frustrations.

If we examine the sources of our conflicts and frustrations, we find that they fall into four general categories.

It is frustrating to have to make a choice between two things that are equally appealing. John wanted to go skiing for the weekend, but he also had the chance to have a date on Saturday night with a new and interesting young lady. He wanted to do both but he could not be in two places at once. He puzzled over the matter for several days and it was a difficult decision because both prospects were equally appealing. No matter which choice he made, he would deprive himself of something he wanted. Most of us develop skills in making decisions of this type, and we learn to live with the simple fact that we are limited in space and time.

It can also be frustrating to have to make a choice between two equally undesirable things. We may dislike going to the dentist, but we have a throbbing toothache. In order to get relief from the toothache, we have to consider going to the dentist. Sometimes the inner mechanisms that govern our behavior can do strange things to us at the decision-making level. Often when the patient gets to the dentist's office, he feels a sense of relief as he sits in the waiting room. He may decide that he does not really need to have his tooth treated after all. Yet if he leaves the dentist's office he may find that the toothache returns shortly thereafter. In the course of life we learn some skills in discriminating between painful alternatives. So we tell the painful truth and accept the consequences because we cannot tolerate the burden of guilt. We have the inoculations that we do not want because we would rather have them and be able to make our trip to Europe than to suffer the consequences of avoiding the simple needle prick.

The type of frustration and inner conflict that grows from ambivalence is particularly difficult to cope with. Here the choice is between alternatives that have built-in conflicts between what is desirable and what is not. Emily had great satisfaction in her career as a journalist. It was exciting and she met interesting people and achieved considerable recognition. Yet there were times when she was lonely and had feelings of unfulfillment. She wanted adventure, and yet she wanted some stability and serenity in her life. When the prospect of marriage confronted her, she was in conflict. She loved a man and wanted to be with him constantly, and she wanted the stability and serenity she thought might come with marriage. But she did not enjoy the prospect of losing her freedom and the excitement of her career. She thought that she could combine some of the advantages with some of the disadvantages, but she was sure that she would have to make changes and adjustments that would end some parts of her life that she did not want to lose. Whatever her decision, life would not be quite the same again.

Wherever there is love, there is ambivalence. We have the benefits and privileges of the love relationship, but we also have the limitations on freedom and the shared responsibility and added obligations that come with investing one's life in the life of another. Many of the frustrations and conflicts of life come where there is intensity of personal commitment. Police records show that most murders and assaults occur among people who have a close personal relationship. Frustration builds up until there is a moment of explosion and the crime of passion is committed. Many of the crises of life are bound up with human relations that promise benefits at the same time that they increase obligations and responsibilities. The choices produce frustrations and conflicts, and coping skills are important for love and marriage.

Perhaps the most difficult types of frustration are bound up with two ambivalence-producing situations. Pity the poor man who is in love with two women and must make a choice between them. Consider the plight of the man who is offered two positions at the same time. He loves the country and has always wanted to live on a ranch, yet he has education debts and needs to pay them off. One teaching position has the benefits of a small western town where he could own his own ranch and live in the country as he always wished, but it does not pay nearly as much as a teaching post in a university in the midst of a great city. He has to make his decision between alternatives that are both appealing and limiting.

Efforts to resolve frustration and conflict may also produce further stress. Frustration may lead to strong desires for emancipation.

The hermit seeks to separate himself from the social conditions that have frustrated his life, but certainly the choice that the hermit makes produces limitations on experience and the possibility for self-fulfillment.

People who have difficulty managing the ambivalence implicit in marriage may seek emancipation as a solution. Yet many have found the legal release of divorce to be less of a release from stress than had been expected. Often it involves moving from one set of frustrations to another that is just as difficult to manage.

All of life is involved in crisis. The skills that we develop emerge from the total experience of the past with all of its previous crises. How we have developed tends to determine how we will function in each new set of circumstances.

As we have seen in this chapter, crises differ in their nature and in their emotional content. But they also differ in what they mean to the person who confronts them. If there has been a long growth of skill in wise management of crises, each new crisis will be seen in perspective and met with skill. But for the person who has been deprived of a chance to develop coping skills, the process of life may present an unending series of frustrations and conflicts that make him nonfunctional.

Human behavior is a complex response to the variety of events in life. Whether the events come to be crises largely depends on how we have learned to live with frustration, conflict, and the need for adjustment.

10

Crises and Personality Development

Through the last nine chapters we have tried to get a clearer picture of what a crisis is, how it develops, and what its characteristics are when observed from various points of view. We started with the observation that there is something about a crisis that can break an individual or stimulate growth and maturity. Only those who are emotionally abnormal appear to be untouched by crises.

We have observed that some crisis situations tend to produce resources for resolving the crises, but that skills developed in managing crises at one level of experience may compound them at another. Coping with a crisis can change the person. So in this chapter we will look more closely at the ways in which crises interact with the personality in its development.

Many forces and influences come together to shape a person. Some of the processes are gentle and subtle. Others are dominant and life-shaking.

Hereditary influences can be a major factor in the types of crises a person must live with. Hereditary factors determine whether a person will be male or female, and life roles and relationships are modified because of sex from the time it is decided whether the new being will be dressed in pink or blue. The toys that are gifts, the attitudes of adults, the gentle guidance, and the subtle expectations are at work early to structure this biological inheritance.

Hereditary conditions determine race, minority status, social stresses. Being born black in the South, Jewish in Nazi Germany, or a Brahmin in India has been a major conditioning force shaping the crises of life. Being born a twin immediately creates psychic, social, and biological problems that may well become crises in time.

The processes of maturation also may produce their share of crises. The pituitary gland is a wonderful part of anyone's basic equipment, for it tends to regulate growth and decide when the growth process has been completed. But an overactive pituitary may go a long way toward deciding the professional career of a boy who grows to be seven feet four inches tall. As soon as the high school basketball coach sees him, unusual influences are employed to shape his career. So with the dwarf who finds his way into the circus.

From the time prenatal influences of diet and deprivation are at work on the unborn child, his maturation has a bearing on what he will eventually become. The child whose mother has inadequate food and medical care during pregnancy may show signs of inadequate mental development as well as symptoms of physical inadequacy.

Environment may also have a bearing on development. A fetus whose mother is infected with Rubella may experience a physical and social crisis for years to come because of this environmental impingement on his life. One out of every sixteen babies born in the United States suffers from some defect that could prove a handicap to his normal development.

The emotional environment also may have significant and critical impact on personality development. A fractured family, a war-disrupted family life, an economic depression, or other events that threaten the emotional security of a child's early environment may have a distressing impact on his maturation.

The atmosphere of violence may so impinge upon life that the early years are surrounded with fear and anxiety. Fear of bullies on a school bus or of violence in the school yard may interfere with the educational process. The world of a child surrounded by fear and anxiety may be so reduced that he is deprived of many healthful influences.

The chance for healthy and vigorous interaction between the vital force of the individual and his world is basic to sound growth. When this interaction is impeded, something within the individual is never realized and he is critically deprived at the point of his growth into self-confidence and self-acceptance.

Those who work with personality growth affirm that there is yet another dimension that is hard to define and fits none of the categories mentioned above, yet is constantly visible to those who look deep into the mystery of personality development. It is called mysticism by some, and the third force or third world by others. Whatever its name, it represents some integration of being beyond the merely physical and psychological. It is the point where superconscious forces are at work to produce the individual's optimum functioning, what Abraham Maslow, in *Motivation and Personality,* calls the peak experience of human consciousness. While many aspects of heredity and environment may produce crises, there is a level of human experience that produces maximum competence in coping with all that life may bring.

While developmental processes tend to move from the simple to the complex, from disorganization to integration, from fragmented experience to organized perception, it is also important to realize that the human consciousness has within itself the capacity to find the high level of self-realization and fulfillment that can activate the superhealthy being, the person who knows and sustains the peak experience.

The developmental process of individual personality growth needs to be explored in order to see how we can effect change and achieve useful forms of adaptation. How do we learn, really?

Because such importance is given to formal education, we tend to think much of our learning takes place in classrooms. While we may gain factual information in schools, the skills for living are more apt to be taught in other ways.

Much of our learning takes place through the gradual but constant processes of conditioning. We experience a stimulus and respond to it. The repeated response sets up patterns of behavior that are habitual. Much of what we learn is built into the habit patterns of life and so remains largely outside the area of intelligent examination. This is just the way we do things, and we may have inherited these habit patterns from those around us.

Much of our basic skill for living is learned in a high chair university. In order to get what we need from life, we soon learn techniques for adaptation and adjustment. We learn how to make our needs known to others, and we learn to read the subtle and nonverbal responses that tell us what others are thinking and feeling. We learn what will bring approval and the little bonuses of life. We also learn what will bring disapproval and hostility. So we learn early in life to suppress certain behaviors and to express vigorously the feelings we have learned will be acceptable.

Some of what we learn is in the realm of problem-solving. We learn what will work and what will not by trial and error. We don't designate it as such, for at that stage we are not inclined to use concepts. But we get the idea by the different ways people respond to various actions. So also we explore the world of things. We find some things are heavy and others light, some hard and others soft, some taste good and others do not. So by a process of selection on the basis of experimentation we discover for ourselves some practical skills in doing things and using things.

So it is that we learn a language. We test some sounds and measure the response. We hear others speak and copy the sounds they make. We find that we get quick and precise results when we are able to use the right words, and the rewards are so significant that we find it worthwhile to develop special skills in the use of sounds and word symbols.

We also learn motor skills: We can make our muscles work for us, we can walk and run, we can play games, and we can coordinate a variety of muscle systems to accomplish the things we want. But when we become mobile we also learn that there are places we cannot go and things we cannot touch. So our skills at one point may create crises at another.

We also learn emotional behavior. We learn the responses that are appropriate for pleasure and pain, and we learn to respond to the feelings of others. So we smile when they smile and feel frightened when they are frightened. When we are young we are completely at the mercy of those around us, so it becomes important for us to be responsive to their feelings. But if their feelings are unhealthy we may learn forms of emotional behavior that will be difficult to outgrow with time. Yet if we are surrounded with love we can learn to accept it and ourselves, and to respond to others freely and with affection.

Some of our learned skills will be social. We will try to please others for the rewards that are implicit. So we will learn that it is more acceptable to eat with care and avoid spilling. We will learn to manage doors and clothes and table utensils. We will learn to differentiate the roles of those around us—parental, familial, authoritative. We may well learn prejudices and modes of approval from those around us.

Moral values will also be learned indirectly as well as directly. We will be told what is right and wrong, but we will also learn what we can get away with. We will begin to make distinctions between bad and good, smart and stupid, accepted and unaccepted. In this way we will begin to get an idea about ourselves, as to whether we are loved or unloved, approved or disapproved, wanted or unwanted. Also we will learn ways of protecting ourselves from disappointment, disapproval, and punishment. So we may learn to deceive, to hide the consequences of our acts and blame others. At that point our social and moral education makes way for healthy and unhealthy adaptations and adjustments.

Some of the important lessons we learn both directly and indirectly are related to our skills in adjusting to others. We interact with others constantly and learn subtle and blatant forms of adaptations according to what suits our needs. Some adaptations avoid crises and others precipitate them.

Maladaptive behavior tends to create crises. John enjoyed singing and playing his guitar. He decided to drop out of college and use his inheritance to become a traveling troubadour. He was sure he would be discovered, make a series of hit records, and become rich and famous. But his talent was limited and in a highly competitive form of entertainment he never made it. It was fun for a while, but it was maladaptive behavior to misjudge his talent and engage in a course of action that seemed to invite frustration and failure.

Joe was not clear in his perception of relationships. He was a friend of the boss and they shared drinks together on various occasions. There was a clear plant rule against drinking during working hours. But Joe depended on his friendship with the boss. When others warned him, he paid no attention. When he was fired for drinking during working hours, he was confused. He had so emphasized the friendship of his boss that he had gotten everything else out of perspective. He had learned the value of friendship, but he had learned it out of the context of employment and had difficulty making the necessary adjustment. So his faulty understanding led to a self-destructive form of adaptation.

In the process of personality development it is important not only to learn valid behavior patterns but also to learn that what is appropriate for one set of circumstances may be inappropriate for another. Most people tend to learn rather quickly when their way of doing things is unacceptable to others and they readily seek to adapt and adjust. But when learning has been faulty and perception inadequate, the ability to modify may be impaired. A defensive stance may take the place of adaptation, and self-injury may be compounded.

The basic drives of life—biological, emotional, and social—must be met in a context of acceptable behavior for a person to develop his individuality within bounds and at the same time maintain the structure of socially valid living. So he seeks a growth pattern that permits both personal fulfillment and social responsibility within the framework he chooses for his life.

Deprivation may be a useful part of the process of learning

to cope with crises. Whenever a choice is made, a person must deprive himself of one alternative. But practice in meeting the disappointments that go with making choices helps the development of coping skills.

Many parents who grew up during the great depression of 1929–35 determined to make sure that their children did not go through such misery. Whenever their children asked for anything, they were given it. The parents were providing a life devoid of the type of disappointment necessary in learning to manage deprivation. The parents confused deprivation with destitution. In order to protect their children from destitution, they denied them the chance of learning to cope with reasonable limitations.

Many young people who grew to maturity during years of affluence were denied the opportunity to learn through the choices that come with minor crises. So they did not have the slowly built resources to cope with major crises. When faced with major frustration, more than a few moved into a state of despair that was overtly self-destructive.

Civilization is a late development in man's long pilgrimage. People have a built-in need to struggle and develop skills in managing conflict and frustration. It is important to have some ways of heightening our skills in life as we contend with adversity.

There are times when a person can actually be pulled out of depression and despair by having to contend with a crisis. Some unused resource can be brought into action to make him glad he is alive and ready to struggle for something he considers important.

Life is dependent upon adequate meaning for its existence. When meaning fails, life fails. When the basic drives of life remain frustrated, life becomes empty. We can see how important it is, then, to learn to grow with our crises, to develop skills in adaptation and adjustment, and to use our times of stress to develop resources for managing crises. Our processes of growth are seldom even and well-balanced, but it is not always the easy or smooth path that takes us to our goals. It may well be the skill we learn in coping with our crises that brings us our greatest maturity, our deepest perception, and our finest self-realization.

11

Crises of Early Childhood

Children have deep feelings but they are not able to talk about them. Because of their complete dependency on others during the early stages of life, children are highly vulnerable. This vulnerability can produce stress and significant crises that can have bearing on all the rest of life.

How then can we learn about what is going on in the child? One major way is to explore deep psychological patterns of behavior as they are reflected in literature and biographical material. The literature of childhood illuminates the moods of the child's inner life and also sheds light on the other three methods of discovering the child's inner world.

Studies of nursery rhymes reveal that these simple forms of literature are resonant to the needs and interests of the child. They speak in familiar and comfortable ways about the things that can distress a child. Learning to walk and manage his body against the pull of gravity is a large adventure for the youngster, and it is reassuring to know that others have had the same problems. So Jack and Jill and their misfortunes make welcome company in the little ventures that can seem so big to a child.

The child often seems at a disadvantage, for he knows so little about so many things. His need for reassurance is nourished by taking the simple things of life and glorifying them. So Jack

Horner pulls out a plum and becomes a good boy. And Little Miss Muffet may be frightened of a spider but feels better when she is able to put her fear into words.

Let us look at two longer children's stories to see what they tell us about the emotional crises of young children. The first is Jack and the Beanstalk, and the second is Hansel and Gretel.

Jack is a poor boy with no father and a mother who is frustrated and so anxiety-ridden that she has trouble making ends meet and often takes out her anger on Jack by scolding him for his inadequacy as a substitute man about the house. When the economic plight of Jack's mother becomes acute, she entrusts him with their last valuable possession, the family cow. He is to sell it for money needed to buy food.

But Jack is young, naive, and obviously not acquainted with matters of the marketplace. Some people would call him stupid (a judgment his mother would certainly concur in). So Jack goes off with the cow only to encounter a sociopathic individual so lacking in conscience he even takes advantage of a helpless child. He persuades Jack to trade the cow for a bag of beans. When Jack returns home with the few beans, his mother is deeply distressed and ventilates her feelings in such a way that Jack feels personally rejected. He is reduced in his own sight, and desperately in need of some way to restore his status in regard to his mother.

Jack is at an age when magical thinking is common—and at this point a little magic would serve him well. The story provides it in large measure. The beans his mother has thrown out the window in disgust and anger begin to grow miraculously. The first day they are up to Jack's knees, and the second up to his shoulders. When he points this out to his mother she is in no mood to listen to such weird tales. But the beans keep on growing magically until they go up out of sight into the clouds.

Jack has a large emotional investment in the beans. He feels a strong impulse to explore where they lead him, so he starts to climb the beanstalk, going higher and higher, up into the clouds. On the other side of the clouds he comes upon a kingdom of giants who possess great treasure. The mother giant, really kind at heart although of threatening size, is overruled by the father giant, who does not take kindly to the little fellow —who has just stolen his valuables. He chases Jack, but Jack manages to escape and climbs back down his beanstalk. So pleased is Jack's mother with the treasure he has brought that Jack decides to repeat the exploit. He is now making his mother happy, a pleasant contrast to the earlier scolding and aspersions on his intelligence.

Jack's repeated visits to the kingdom of the giants continue to produce treasures that make his mother happy, but as with most magical circumstances, there comes a time when they no longer work. The giant becomes so angry at Jack that he tries to follow him down the beanstalk. But the beanstalk was intended for Jack and no one else, and the weight of the giant is too much for it. Jack helps the matter along with his little hatchet, and the giant falls to his death. Since things have been looking up for Jack and his mother, they really don't need any more treasures from the giant's realm. They can now make it on their own and, as is usually the case in stories of this kind, they are able to live with skills in managing crises ever after.

What kinds of crises in a child's life does this story cover? It deals with the threat of poverty, a fractured family, emotional insecurity, a frustrated mother, a son who is expected to be more mature and competent than his years or experience warrant, accusations of failure and stupidity, and a feeling of personal inadequacy at the point of family need. If you stop to think about it, this is quite a burden for a simple children's story about a young boy. If we were to be more analytical in approach, we might discern many other elements in the human relations among the characters. But for our purposes let us look at the story in its simpler meanings.

How does Jack resolve the problems of his life as revealed in the story? He does not directly reject the judgments of others about his stupidity and inadequacy, but rather seeks to employ magical powers to prove that not only can he do anything that a man can do but he is even able to outsmart a giant. He proves to himself and to his mother that he is worth having around.

His cleverness is matched only by his loving devotion to his mother. Once he has proved that, they can live happily ever after in wealth and security. Such is the fantasy world of the child as he attempts to compensate for his smallness and weakness. Fantasy can serve a useful purpose during the time when he must adapt and adjust to the world of big people, but it becomes a hazard if he prefers it to reality during later phases of his development.

In the story of Hansel and Gretel, in its many forms, there is a basic theme that appears without variation. Two children who have resolved their sibling rivalry live together in complete freedom in a wonderful world that they can explore to their heart's content. There is no one around to tell them what they can or cannot do.

But this state of complete freedom has its limitations when mealtime comes. Hunger drives them toward home and the person who presides over the kitchen. But no matter how hungry they may be, they see this creature of the kitchen as threatening and able to exert a witch's power over them. The voice of the old witch grates on their nerves and if she didn't have such a hold over them, they would try to get away from her.

Hansel and Gretel watch the old witch at work and are frightened to see the things she throws into the big kettle. When a chicken is plucked, its skin looks very much like that of a little person. Even the witch's chuckle as she adds the ingredients becomes menacing if you are not sure you will not be next. The blazing fire, the uncomfortable heat, the menacing look, the grating voice, and the threatening size and demeanor of the old witch suggest the view the child may have of those who would limit his freedom at the same time that they exert a powerful control over him because of his basic dependency. How he would like to escape from the threatening control, but how chained he is by his limited resources for independent life.

The child must contend with his small size in a world of giants. He must contend with his limited experience and knowledge in the midst of those who seem all-knowing. He feels a need to prove himself but has little or nothing to prove himself with. The ground is set for severe internal conflicts as he tries to verify his value and establish a base for self-acceptance and self-realization.

During the years of growth into self-awareness he has powerful forces to contend with. He must learn the social graces by observation and trial and error. He must learn a language with no grammar or vocabulary to start with. He must learn the skills of body control even though the muscles may not be quite ready for the kind of control that is required of him. He must cope with ethical patterns that are set by others and that seem cruel efforts to frustrate his life energy rather than to appreciate it.

The crises that beset his life come on so rapidly that there is little chance to consolidate his gains. The pain of birth is followed by the task of learning to see, where the upside-down images are put into their proper perspective. Then there is the problem of clarifying and adjusting to the big people who have all power over him. When he has just learned to manage sucking at a breast properly, he has the pain of teething and the troublesome deprivations that come with weaning and the need to learn new techniques of eating.

Just as the young child feels he has gained some victories in the learning process, it may all be shaken by the arrival of a new creature who takes center stage. Then the adults around him begin to function in ways that are confusing and threatening. These big people make a fuss and give their attention to a little person who cannot do any of the things he has learned through a long and sometimes painful learning process. The new baby cannot eat or walk or talk or do useful things, yet he gets more than his share of attention. What can the older child do to regain his place in the love and attention of the family? He can make a special effort for attention by becoming noisy and destructive. Or he may regress to types of behavior that obviously warrant attention. Here in this process of coping with the loss of security he may establish patterns that will be called neurotic behavior in time to come.

The young child is beset by a variety of demands in the

socialization process. When he uses the trial and error method of learning, he may be punished by parents who do not understand the difficult process he is engaged in. He may become uncertain about what he is supposed to do when parents show ambivalence toward him. His experience may add to the normal concerns of early childhood the unhealthy emotions that are transmitted by unstable parents or other adults, and his chance to become a competent person may be impaired.

At Yale with Gesell, Ilg, and Ames, large numbers of children have been observed to establish patterns of normal behavior. At Princeton and formerly in Europe Jean Piaget has done intensive observation of children to establish how they develop skills, controls, values, and personal competence. These extensive observations indicate that the child's growth is in large measure governed by natural laws, and constantly modified by the circumstances that structure the natural life force.

Extensive experimentation under controlled conditions of diet, emotional climate, and human relationships have led to the tentative conclusion that child development can be enhanced by some conditions and impaired by others. Studies of twins under different environmental conditions and different external influences show how conditioning forces modify the child's character and behavior.

Studies of free association, dream analysis, hypnotically controlled regression, and the evaluation of clinical data in psychotherapeutic processes make it clear that many of the crises that trouble adults can be traced back to times in early childhood when the natural, healthy direction of life was diverted.

While it is difficult to be sure of what is going on in the thoughts and feelings of a young child, it is obvious that imaginative methods by ingenious researchers have illuminated the subject for us. It is equally important for us to know that progress has been made in therapeutic intervention with young children. There are ways to prevent traumatic experience in young children. There are also significant forms of intervention to relieve the impact of crises after they have been experienced.

Prevention and treatment of crisis situations can be summarized under three general headings: treatment of the social environment, treatment of the child, and treatment of the parents.

Let us first consider the social environment, which is part of the natural setting for growth. When the family structure is sound, the child is fortified so that he can move into and out of crises with the type of growth momentum that sustains the forward motion of his life. When the social structure is faulty, that structure can be modified. In some cases a substitute home can be provided. In others a specialized climate for living can be afforded by a treatment center. There are specialized institutions for severely damaged children to meet the special needs and constant demands that the family setting cannot be expected to provide.

Second, the psychological treatment of children has been developed in recent decades and significant gains in the management of crises can be provided. Play therapy has probably been one of the more important resources for treatment of the disturbed child. Here with simple toys and under careful observation the child is able to express his full range of feelings in a way that the skilled observer can understand and direct. Anger can be worked out through the fingers by using modeling clay, trust can be developed by being in the presence of an adult who is totally accepting of behavior, stimulation is found in having someone who will listen to everything you say. All these give direction to the natural move toward health. When started early enough, the psychological methods used in child guidance centers can prevent deep disturbance and resolve the stresses that may make a child nonfunctional.

Third, and one of the important resources, is the treatment of parents so that they can better understand the child's behavior and the symptoms of his emotional states. In the constant interrelation of child and parent, important changes can be brought about by a change in parental attitude. Often crisis intervention is as much a matter of helping to relieve the adults' anxiety about a child's behavior as it is a direct approach to the child's disturbance. Parents can talk about their children's problems in a group setting that shares and reduces their anxiety at the same time that they are gaining increased competence in understanding and accepting the meaning of the child's behavior. The benefits here, of course, can be cumulative, for the skills learned can be passed on to other children and to other generations of parents.

New insights into the needs of young children are helpful in getting relief from stress at an earlier age. In the child guidance clinic where I worked, during a six-year period the average referral age was reduced from eleven to five. Instead of waiting for abnormal behavior to become a serious community problem with the adolescent and preadolescent, parents and teachers observed and reacted to the needs of the young child in nursery school and early grades. In this way the burdens of anxiety and stress were reduced, and the children were given the chance for more normal and healthy development.

It is important for all of us to appreciate and use the new diagnostic and treatment facilities that are being provided for children who are suffering from crises in their lives. The earlier they can be helped, the longer will be their opportunity to benefit from professional and community services that can serve their special needs.

12

Crises of the Older Child

For the older child, five to ten for girls and six to eleven for boys, life can be wonderfully interesting or quite disturbing. He can begin to develop untold possibilities or he can begin to struggle with large troubles.

The older child knows a world that is rapidly expanding in every direction. He now has a clear sense of time and space. He knows the next block, the next town, and often in this generation the next state or country. He has had a chance to see people of different cultures and races, and may have had personal encounters that become the basis for comparisons and contrasts.

With the mobility that is a part of our culture, he may well have lived in two or three quite different places. He may have had a chance to attend more than one school and have some basis for deciding what he likes or does not like, what kinds of people he feels comfortable with and what kinds he would rather avoid.

Some of the aura of omnipotence that surrounded his parents may have been dimmed by comparison. He may not be so sure that his father is stronger than any other man on the block. He may compare things said by his teacher and his mother and be perplexed by their disagreements. He may compare what he learns in science classes with what he hears at home and be troubled by discrepancies.

The older child is aware of the social context of life. If he hears an argument between his father and mother in the quiet hours of the night, his security may be shaken for he can be fearful about what would happen if his home were broken by conflict. He has been concerned about other children whose parents were killed in accidents, for he wondered who would take care of the orphans. He wonders what might happen to him in a family crisis and is constantly aware of social threats and the need for reassurance.

His world is extended by television, news reports, geography, and social science studies. The larger the world becomes, the more possibility there seems to be for earthquakes, tornadoes, floods, and life-threatening calamities. While he may not seem to be paying attention to these things, they are slowly but surely becoming a part of his awareness.

During these periods of awareness and growth his personality is developing. He may become more anxious about all the things he discovers in his larger world, or he may become more secure as he sees the confidence of others who have learned to manage crises with skill and competence.

The older child can also learn that life can be filled with fun, interesting things to do, and pleasures to be enjoyed. He may find that he can travel through reading, or enjoy music that he creates himself or shares with others. He may begin to play musical instruments, which can make him eligible for a school band or orchestra with all the excitement and satisfaction that can come from creative group activity.

For the older child life can be opening up to wonder and appreciation. The world of nature may intrigue him endlessly and he may become an amateur scientist collecting all kinds of shells, stones, bird nests, and flowers, or stamps, coins, and pictures of astronauts and football stars. His individuality begins to assert itself in the things he enjoys, explores, and becomes proficient in managing. He may enjoy making and saving or spending money and show business inclinations at an early age.

During this period of later childhood there seems to be a time when some life forces are held in check to allow for consolidation and socialization. In comparison with other forms of animal life this consolidation period is an important resource for social achievement. Cats, dogs, elephants, and bears begin to reproduce biologically at about one-twelfth of their expected life span. But humans with their longer period of social adjustment and development usually are capable of reproduction at about one-fifth of the expected life span. The major difference here not only allows for increased education and learned social skills but also provides important opportunities for the personality to develop coping skills that are necessary for carrying on the life of the race.

Some of the areas of interest and exploration may be fraught with hazards of misunderstanding and punishment. Young children have a great interest in their bodies and how they function. This leads to self-examination and experimentation. It also leads to the exploration and examination of the bodies of other persons, especially those who appear to be different. Left to themselves, children will engage in this form of exploration until their curiosity is satisfied, and they will learn the differences between black and white, male and female, circumcised and uncircumcised. Should their explorations be misunderstood and punishment employed, the whole subject may become far more interesting and the impulse toward voyeuristic activity may be inadvertently encouraged.

This is also the age when children are interested in the sex relations of their parents. They wake up in the night and wonder what is going on and how to interpret what they see or hear. If they break in on their parents at an inappropriate moment, they may be scolded so severely that they transfer their anxiety to all things related to sex and suffer from disturbances about sexual behavior for long periods of time.

This period may also be one of health hazards. This is the time when the contagious illnesses of childhood usually strike if not controlled by immunization. This is the time of frequent broken bones, arms, and legs. This is the time when psychogenic ailments may show up with asthma and other forms of respiratory diseases. It may be the time of infected tonsils and rheumatic fever. It also may be the time for allergies to manifest themselves, along with headaches and stomach distress. But in spite of the hazards that show themselves this period of personality consolidation is usually marked by good health and high vitality and energy.

Emotions are always elusive, but with the older child there may be even more difficulty than usual in bringing emotions into focus. The easy crying of early childhood is past; in its place are strong impulses to deny or repress feelings. Yet they are always there and often baffling. They may be observed in the very forms of behavior that are at work to try to obscure feelings. Rapid blinking of eyes, biting of the lips, jerky motions of arms and legs tend to indicate tension and strong emotions. Sometimes children are punished for crying as well as for doing the things they substitute for crying. Emotions exist and have their own validity. It is important to understand the process that produces them rather than assault the manifestations of the feelings. During these years the child is trying to learn how to cope with life in large terms. This assignment may stimulate strong feelings. The expression of these feelings provides clues to how the process of coping with life may be going for the child.

Some indications of how the struggle to manage the larger world is going may show up in the ways fears are expressed. Often this is through dreams. Dreams show what is going on in the individual beyond his words and daily activity. The powerful anxiety dreams of childhood are called nightmares. These may be triggered by struggles for adequacy, but they also tend to reflect an age-old struggle against the forces of nature, the wild beasts, and the big people who surround and threaten the child. The dream life of the child indicates some of the reorganizing and consolidating effort that is at work. When life and dreams are frightening, it is important to have calm and quiet big people nearby to whom one can turn for love, comfort, and reassurance.

Most of the problems we have in life are with people. The older child is deeply involved in the process of learning to get along with a large variety of new people. His enlarged world includes the people he encounters in school, church, clubs, stores, and the general community. He sees people who exploit, bully, threaten, and antagonize. He also sees people who listen, appreciate, accept, and understand. He sets some of the models that may stay with him for life, for he decides how he will relate to people. He begins to decide whether he will value people and work with them, or distrust them and work against them.

During these years the older child develops a clearer sense of selfhood. He thinks about himself, talks about himself, and compares himself with others. He may be sensitive to criticism for he considers it an assault on his growing self-concept which is not yet strong enough to tolerate much criticism. Yet he can be responsive to reason and highly cooperative when the invitation for cooperation is managed with appreciation for him as a person. This is the time when he likes to be chosen first to play on a team. If he is not chosen, he can quietly retreat into himself to nurse his emotional wounds.

Children engage in experimental living through their play. This is an essential part of their growth in competence. They play to gain competence in muscle coordination and in forms of group life. They play to manage deep inner resources in the context of their living. They reveal their personal abilities through their play and learn to enjoy the skills they possess and retreat from situations that reveal their incompetence. So if they are poorly coordinated they may leave the playground for the swimming pool where their skills are more adequate. They may want adult companionship in their play and constantly give the invitation, "Come play with me." They may play at cooking and child care with dolls. Even professional skills may be anticipated by playing doctor, teacher, or engineer. Play often becomes so strenuous at this age that excessive fatigue may be a problem.

Each new generation or decade makes education more complex, for there are always new and important things to learn. Because our society is so complex, a child has a great deal to learn before he can begin to function in it. Some of what he learns in school is more significantly related to attitudes than to information. When young children see adults assaulting a school bus in a racial conflict, we can be sure those children learned more that day about people than about spelling. When a child is thrust into a new and frightening environment, he may be called upon to employ more skills for adjustment than he possesses. If he cannot cope with this, he may retreat into himself with feelings of defeat and self-injury. These are years when the child develops increased coordination between his feelings and his words for describing them. This makes him more accessible for psychotherapy.

During these years the child also is expected to develop a working code of ethical and moral values. Society is built on our self-governing response to group needs. There cannot be a policeman assigned to every person to govern his behavior. Most of the time most people must function according to a practical code that protects others and themselves. So a child is expected to develop some idea of the rights of others, the nature of discipline, respect for people and their possessions, a sense of justice, forgiveness and restitution, and kindness, mercy, and goodwill. Along with these positive feelings he develops a capacity to feel guilt, to become uncomfortable when he violates his code and self-discipline. His capacity for feeling shame may develop more in relation to his own group than to the adults in his life. During this stage he may function by a code within a code.

During these years the child begins to develop some concepts that have a philosophical flavor about them. His sense of justice and his need for integrity are actively expressed. He is angry if falsely accused, and feels insecure if others deceive him. He is now mature enough to confront the meaning of illness, desertion, and death. He begins to organize his life around some ideas that he has tested and found useful.

We can see that there are important strengths developing within the life of the older child. He is becoming a distinct person in his own right. But he is also moving through personal and social conditions that can produce crises. These times of crisis may be important for the rest of his life because he has not yet developed strengths to manage large crises without help. Yet he may have difficulty signaling to others his need for special help. Fortunately the number of people with skills in observing the behavior that signals such needs is increasing, but the facilities available in many communities are still so limited that many children are obliged to make it on their own.

When a child runs into trouble in managing his crises, it usually shows up first in his behavior. He may not be able to function in school. He daydreams. He sits and looks out the window endlessly, and when the teacher calls his name it is as if he hears her speaking from far off through a long tunnel.

Willy was brought to the guidance center by a guidance counselor because he had stopped functioning adequately in school. The change had come about shortly after his father died of a heart attack while off on a business trip. Relatives had whisked Willy out of the house as soon as the news came. For a week he was in an unfamiliar environment with many questions and few answers that he could accept—for he sensed that he was being deceived. When he returned home a week later, he often found his mother crying. When he asked questions, he was told that it was nothing he need worry about. But he did worry. He knew something had happened to his father but he did not know what. He began to make assumptions. He had not always behaved as he should. He had done things behind his father's back that he knew he should not do. He began to assume that his father was so angry about his behavior that he had left home without even saying goodbye. His guilt feelings began to grow to intolerable proportions and there was no one he could talk with about them.

Finally in the accepting atmosphere of the clinic Willy began to pour out his concerns and go back to do the unfinished work of his encounter with tragic and untimely death. It was easier for him to cope with death than with deceit about it. His crisis was managed when he was allowed to confront it with help and within his own framework of ideas and feelings.

Often adults compound crises for older children by reading their own thoughts and feelings into the lives of their children. Children feel and respond at the level of their development. It is important to let them confront life crises at the point of their competence and experience.

The child who faces the stresses that are part of minority status needs help to see them in social rather than personal terms. The child who grows up in a sick family needs to learn that the behavior he observes is part of human inadequacy and social illness rather than a judgment against himself. Children are quick to suspect desertion or abandonment, as if they had been unworthy of love and acceptance. They need to see that adult behavior is often the result of the adults' inadequacy rather than any failure on the child's part.

When children at this age begin to compare themselves with others in abilities and skills, those who are handicapped or deprived in obvious ways become doubly vulnerable. They not only have extra problems in the developmental process but they also have to struggle against the psychic wounds that may come with their feelings of inadequacy. But children during these years can accept a challenge. They can learn that, through no fault of their own, they must be extra competent to compete. So they can learn to use their limitations as a resource rather than a form of cruelly imposed defeat.

In coping with the crises of these important years, the child has developed skills that make more precise forms of therapeutic help possible. Psychotherapy that employs language skills may now be used in conjunction with play therapy. Group therapy procedures may be used to stimulate the dynamic forces of group identity and the challenge of group participation. Also, increasingly, environmental resources can be brought into use through family-centered therapy, through special schools with a therapeutic environment, and through institutions that are designed and staffed to cope with the more serious crises that may show themselves during this period of life.

13

Crises of Adolescence

Adolescence has long been considered a time of turbulence
and emotional crises. The turbulent era in which we live can
make it doubly so. What is there about adolescence that makes
it such a difficult time?

There is an assumption implicit in this question that may not
be warranted. Adolescence does not have to be a time of painful
adjustment and stress. Many people grow through this period
of rapid change with inner adequacy and important personality
development. Others find resources to help manage stresses
they could not easily manage alone.

During the years of adolescence several important life processes coincide. First there is a rapid change in the glandular
system. Hormones pour into the system at a rapid rate. There
are important physical changes in a relatively short time. With
boys, the voice changes, hair grows over major areas of the
body, muscles develop, and sex characteristics become pronounced. With girls, body lines are modified, breasts develop,
and physical manifestations of sex differentiation become more
pronounced. Boys and girls become physically men and
women.

Social changes also take place. The peer group's social and
moral values tend to take precedence over those of the nurtur-

ing home. Often this can release strong conflict between parents and their offspring. Parents may feel threatened by the independent actions and attitudes of their children, even though they realize these changes are necessary. Along with these changes goes a more objective attitude toward parents. Increasingly they are seen not as sages and seers but as people with their own problems and limitations. When parents become aware of this they may feel threatened; they may be unprepared to lose their parent mystique and be reduced to merely mortal status.

Psychological change also becomes evident. The rapid changes within the body have their emotional counterparts. New sensitivities develop. New urges assert themselves. Because there is no personal history of these feelings and their control, the adolescent is apt to be overwhelmed by what is going on deep inside him. He may have the idea that he is feeling emotions unique in human history, that no one can understand him because no one else has ever experienced what he has. So he may retreat into his inner world, go to his room and close the door, to remain long hours in solitude trying to understand what is happening within him.

At the same time that he is contending with rapid change and turmoil within, he is also struggling with an outer world that seems insensitive to his needs and increases pressures for performance when he least feels like performing. Because he is apparently big and strong, he is expected to work and produce, although he is using up so much energy in his rapid growth that he has little left over for useful labor. Often he is judged to be lazy or unwilling to do his share. And because he cannot figure out his own feelings, he is more apt to show unreasonable anger than he is to give a coherent explanation or defense of himself.

These important influences are at work at one and the same time to complicate life for the adolescent. How can he be understood and helped to cope with his turbulence? Insight into the adolescent problems comes from a wealth of clinical material. Also, new insights emerge from the comparative study of cultures. Important studies have been done of the ways in which people move from childhood into adulthood among the American Indians and in South Sea island cultures as well as in African and European societies. Some cultures with very different ways of doing things have learned skills that we may well examine to improve our understanding.

Some studies of adolescent behavior have grown from a concern about deviant or delinquent and antisocial attitudes of teenagers. They have revealed that at least some of the disturbing behavior is rooted in traumatic experience that may have occurred years before. Rollo May, in his study of anxiety, found that most teenagers in trouble with themselves and others had lost a parent or a person who was a parent equivalent during the first three years of life. Geoffrey Gorer found similarly that much vandalism was an acting out of grief among adolescents who had not been able to manage the acute emotional crisis. Other studies verify these findings and make it rather clear that the aggressive behavior of adolescence may be a restatement or recapitulation of the emotional states of early childhood, expressed with more muscle but still without clear focus. As is apt to be the case with the study of sick behavior, it reveals much about the abnormal but it does not always illuminate the behavior of those who are well within the framework of healthy responses.

A more positive approach to adolescence and its problems and privileges sees it as a time for experimentation, practice, and testing to determine valid directions for growth. While the period may be turbulent, it need not be destructive. It may put stress upon the life of the teenager and those around him, but it may be a stress that stimulates growth toward competence and maturity.

Often adults are uncomfortable about the characteristics that sometimes appear with adolescence. Language is affected and words may be weighted with crude biological references. The adolescent may be trying, through experimentation with language, to come to terms with deep urges that cannot easily be managed. He may be more quarrelsome as he projects his inner conflicts out into his family circle. But this is actually an expression of confidence, for he tends to control his behavior with others, letting it break through only among those he feels love him enough to take all there is of him.

Some of the behavior tends to project inner strife outward into visible forms. He may show aggression against himself by biting his nails. He may develop ordered, compulsive rituals that he performs constantly—as if through them he can control the internal disorder he feels. These activities are usually temporary and are efforts of the emerging ego to bind and control the anxiety that is discomforting. Sometimes the acting out of aggression is given valid social status, and the members of the football squad may give and receive the equivalent of hostility but do it in such a way that they will be cheered for it rather than accused or punished.

Matters that have to do with diet may complicate the growth process of adolescence, for earlier physical maturation due to high protein intake often extends the time span of adolescence, just at the same time that increased educational requirements prolong the need for a dependent relation upon parents and teachers.

Adolescence is characterized by a mood of narcissism, with the teenager interested primarily in himself, his feelings, his looks, his attire. No matter what he looks at, he sees himself reflected back. No matter what happens around him, he takes it as relating to himself. In a heightened stage of narcissistic behavior a person is responsive to praise and devastated by criticism. Some evidences of narcissism are apt to be treated as antisocial. The adolescent is often thought to be selfish, thinking only of what he wants and what is happening to him. He tends to be touchy, preoccupied with his special interests and tastes in music, styles, and colors. When he is uncertain about his own opinions, he is apt to be overassertive as if he needed to prove something to himself as well as others. Because he is trying to defend his rather shaky self-concept, he may be resistant to the ideas of others and hard to influence, especially by those outside his peer group. Because of his self-centeredness he is apt to think he is the only one who ever felt the way he does; if he falls in love it is the great love of history.

Technically, during this period his emotional energy is to a great extent retracted and reinvested in himself rather than in others. Even his capacity to love is likely to be an extension of his own self-interest; the focus of the love can be easily and quickly shifted, apparently without changing the individual's inner balance.

Narcissism in teenage girls often shows itself in denial and indirect satisfactions. A girl will fall violently in love with an athletic hero and yet never even dare to say hello. Gradually, these inadequate directions of love are replaced with relationships where more of the self is invested in another, as the beginnings of true identity relations begin to take the place of narcissistic emotional activity.

But lest we feel this emotional state is unhealthy, we need to realize that it contains the roots of a healthy sense of selfhood. If a person cannot truly love himself, he can never really love another. Here also the dreams of greatness that can inspire heroic living find their inception. With time some of the dreams will collapse, but they have left their mark. The individual moves toward the goals set by his dreams—or he acts on the sense of failure that occurs when his dreams collapse.

The adolescent is also characterized by a large measure of ambivalence about himself and others. He appears to be in constant fluctuation between opposites. This may show in little things: When asked to go on a family picnic he responds with a blunt negative, yet is the first one in the car when it heads for the beach. He may rage at his parents and yet be in constant need of them. He wants to be independent and dependent at the same time, and appears to see no incompatibility in his demands. He can move quickly from love to hate, from depression to elation. Actually what is taking place deep within his personality is an assertion of the dominance of his own selfhood and a rejection of the control others have exerted over him. It doesn't happen all at once, nor is the process even well balanced, but in time the goal is usually accomplished if the process is allowed to proceed without undue interference.

During the period of ambivalent feelings, the major portion

of the hostile feelings are directed at the family and those close by. They represent restraint, but they also usually represent love and security. So, although the family stands for nothing good—with no taste, no style, no quality—it is always there to return to and gain strength from for the next sortie against the threatening world that is yet to be conquered. In a few years this situation usually changes; when the personality has gained enough inner strength to feel secure with itself, the home and parents are seen in a new context and valued for what they have been all along—models toward maturity and competence.

Some of the more strenuous work of adolescence is involved in building the boundaries of selfhood. In early societies this was so important a ceremony that it was elaborated with community recognition, feasts, and sacred obligations. A person is born into a family biologically but is borne into the adult responsibilities of life with pomp and ceremony—no wonder the music most often used for high school graduations is Elgar's "Pomp and Circumstance." Relatively few and largely insignificant ceremonies now launch the child into adulthood. A confirmation ceremony or a Bar Mitzvah may serve this purpose, but in today's culture the coming of age ceremony is more often a copying of self-destructive adult behavior such as indulging in a popular form of drug addiction or moving out on the highway with a couple of tons of lethal machinery.

Some parents are affronted when their children say they do not want to be kissed anymore. They are saying they want to be treated as adults and not children. This is a time when dry, intellectualized discussions go on endlessly. This use of ideas may be a defense against action with the ideas used experimentally to see if they can stand up against competition. Often the discussions are about generalized abstractions and raise questions for which there can be no real answers. But the adolescent has learned to enjoy abstractions and he may wallow in them endlessly—especially when someone is trying to get him to use his muscle on a useful task.

While few adolescents take up positions at the extremes of behavior, those on the extremes gain the most attention. On one hand is the quiet youth who withdraws into himself and does not allow anything new or threatening into his life. On the other is the youth who, with reckless abandon, breaks through restraints to give full expression to the new drives at work in his nature.

Many of the problems of the adolescent center on his efforts to control and direct the strong sex drives that have suddenly arisen in him. Sex identification is not achieved easily or quickly; often it seems that nature steps in to complicate the problem. The excessive glandular activity may show up in acne, the bane of adolescents, which causes them so much embarrassment. The teenager's body may temporarily take on characteristics that are inappropriate for his sex. Girls and boys may become fat and clumsy and less attractive to the opposite sex. A result of this unattractiveness is a temporary delay of overt sexual activity—which may serve a useful purpose. Engaging in sexual activity before the personality is ready for it psychically can produce persistent instability in relation to sex.

During this time of sexually inappropriate behavior there may be periods of homosexual experimentation. If the anxiety about such experimentation is amplified, it may cause a fixation at the homosexual level that inhibits the individual from moving on to a satisfying heterosexuality. The development of adolescent sexuality should move toward the acceptance and appreciation of the male or female role with all the fulfillment and satisfaction that is a part of mature sexuality.

We see that the very nature of adolescent development may produce crises. Experiments with sex often produce pregnancy, which disrupts the life of the girl and the boy, as well as their child. None of the participants is apt to have a happy experience. Those who have a chance to help adolescents cope with such crises should have as their goal a freedom from judgment and a desire to create as much insight and growth as possible from the untimely process.

Often parents compound the problems of their adolescents by acting out the "deserted parents syndrome." Here parents who have not prepared themselves for the growth of their children beyond their control feel threatened and rejected by each new declaration of independence, whether in words or actions. When parents react from a defensive stance, they say and do things that widen the breach and extend the problem period indefinitely.

The resources for meeting the crises that emerge during adolescence are significant. Adolescents often select other adults outside the family to whom they may talk and from whom they seek guidance. The real parents should not feel threatened by this, for it is a recognition of the need for independence. In some cultures adolescents are encouraged to choose surrogate parents at this time.

When the crises center on experimentation with the dimensions of consciousness, with hallucinogens and drugs that modify or expand consciousness, it is important to realize that this is not new behavior. Adolescents have been doing it for ages with such simple techniques as holding the breath to the point of fainting. Monks have often fasted to modify their consciousness. The lethal effect is an indication of the death anxiety so pervasive in our culture. It is quite irrational to destroy consciousness in order to test its boundaries. The best way to prevent a teenage problem in this area is a large dose of love and acceptance, especially in the first five years of age.

Fortunately, older teenagers have developed enough ego strength so that they participate usefully in psychotherapeutic activity. Those who encounter problems and crises can be helped to grow through them to strength of character and to greater skills for coping with the other crises that are bound to come with time. So, for all concerned, adolescence is a challenge. If the strong drives toward maturity are used wisely and well, doors may be opened to a fuller understanding and a richer life.

14

Crises of Youth

For many of today's youth, a major portion of life will be lived in the twenty-first century. The changes that can be imagined, and some that cannot be envisaged, will be a part of their lives. As today's young adults look at themselves, their world, and their future, they are contemplating crises they have not created but must face.

Youth is the stage of life when an individual has moved through adolescence and become an adult, but has not yet formed the structures that will stimulate or stultify his life for years to come. Technically, it is the time from eighteen to twenty-five years of age; actually the boundaries are more indefinite.

There are major decisions to be made during this period of life and this has always been true. But there are new conditions to contend with today. The privilege of maturity makes demands that can create stress and tension, the stuff of personal crises.

Let us look first at the major decisions that have always been part of the responsibility of youth. Traditionally, this is the time to decide on a career, a sex partner, a philosophy of life, and a value structure.

Just a few generations ago, a young man's decision as to a

vocation, a trade or profession, was rather uncomplicated. If he was brought up on a farm, there was a reasonable possibility that he would become a farmer. If his father was a tradesman, it was likely that he too would learn the trade of a carpenter or cabinet maker. If his father was a professional, it could well be that he also would become a lawyer, teacher, physician, or clergyman.

Much of that has now changed. The infinite variety of professional and vocational choices has so expanded that a young man may spend several years experimenting with different forms of work before he is sure what best suits him. Once, a person might simply wish to become a chemist; there are now over 2,000 specializations in the field of chemistry alone. The range of vocational choice is far more complex, and this is true in almost every field.

For women the condition is comparable. A century ago the normal life plan centered on marriage and a family. Few women thought in terms of a career or profession. Now quite the reverse is true. With equal opportunity legislation, many careers in the professions, trades, and business are so inviting that a woman may not want to confine herself to home and family life.

With increasing concern about inner satisfaction, many young people think self-discovery is the most important task of life. "Vocation" may take second place to the effort to live life to the full in terms of its inner meaning. Having seen parents and other adults spend miserable years at tasks they did not enjoy in order to buy a home and pay for material objects, today's youths may be less interested in material possessions and more interested in achieving satisfactions from the enjoyment of nature, friends, and travel. The old crisis of choosing a way of making a living may be replaced by the new crisis of discovering how to make a life.

New attitudes toward sex are more concerned with discovering the nature of sexual fulfillment than with establishing a permanent relationship with one person of the other sex. Traditionally, youths have been expected to choose a spouse, get married, settle down, raise a family, and live together "until death us do part." When society was stable and the community was small, the pattern for establishing a home was rather clearly set. You fell in love with a person who lived nearby and the love was recognized and confirmed by a community ceremony. The obligations and privileges were established by the society in which you lived, and the crises that developed were within clearly defined bounds.

The attitude toward sex has gone through major changes. Sex is an appetite to be satisfied rather than a drive to be harnessed for social purposes. The widespread use of contraceptives, the availability of abortion, and the modification of sex practices has made the selection of a marriage partner more open and less restrictive. While there may be benefits in the new uses of sexual freedom, there may also be some hazards. We are still too close to new lifestyles and concepts of open marriage to make precise and final judgments. Deeply rooted physical, social, and psychological needs cannot be assessed in relation to new methods of satisfaction without time to understand the impact on the individuals involved.

Many young people still choose to find a mate and marry. But for many others there is now what they consider a significant alternative. In interviews with a number of young people I found a certain pattern to be common. One young man not yet thirty said he had slept with about forty young women during a ten-year period. Some had merely been hitchhikers he picked up on a cross-country trip. They had never met before the pickup and have not met since. While the relationships had complete openness and intimacy, there was no permanence. Other relationships lasted from a month to a year. Sometimes the partners had become tired of each other or just decided to move on. They enjoyed each other when they were together, but casually said goodbye. There was never an intention to make the relation permanent, so there was not enough emotional investment to cause an emotional crisis on separation. There was always someone else coming along. Jealousy never came into play, for the same reason.

For someone who has been enslaved by a permanent and

burdensome commitment, this idea of sex without love or commitment may seem a desirable alternative. However, it is worth considering the personality development that coincides with this form of uncommitted relationship. Is this a reversion to primitive forms of social relationship? Or possibly a prolonging of the experimentation of adolescence, a postponement of the personal and social responsibility implicit in any deep human relationship? Has some significant capacity for relationship remained undeveloped, possibly to create crises in the middle years when the desire for adventure and experimentation is superseded by the need for stability and commitment?

Man's capacity for relationships has been built up over a long time. Could it be that in a short period of rapid change we are losing what was so long in the making? Or will we discover a new and freer form of human relationship that makes it possible for people to share intimacy with others without the burdens that used to accompany it? Can we find freedom from hypocrisy yet still maintain that true relationship which is apparently essential to sexual fulfillment at the level of peak human experience?

Contemporary youths, like their predecessors, need a philosophical base for living. Questions are asked—what is the meaning of life and what is really important for me in my period of existence? The answers that come are the basis for a way of life. Old answers that came straight out of the catechism no longer seem valid. The questioners may now find their answers from an Indian guru, or a psychologically focused invitation to discover the true self buried deep within the being.

Much that has been traditional is being jettisoned in favor of selfhood. Given this planet earth with its resources and problems, and my own nature with its needs and opportunities, how can I find a life that makes it possible for me, in the years at my disposal, to live as fully and creatively as possible? How can I enrich the life of man in general and at the same time realize my own potential? Such are the questions asked by many young people today. The philosophical systems of youth appear to be practical, personal, and pertinent to his life.

Yet the struggle for an adequate philosophy of life has built-in difficulties. Among many of the young people with whom I have explored these matters, there seems to be a mood of almost constant low-level depression and generalized confusion. Well educated and mentally and physically well endowed, they would seem to have the ingredients of a good life, yet they have difficulty in putting it together. Freedom is much in demand, but there is not always a clear direction for its use.

One evening we sat around the ample dining table in our Vermont farmhouse with four young people. We were talking of life and its meaning. One of the men had a Ph.D. in classical literature from Harvard. Another had a graduate degree in the study of the Rhineland mystics. One of the women was the daughter of a former cabinet member, and the other was the daughter of a football coach at one of the U.S. service academies. All were attractive, healthy, and intelligent. Their ideal for the present seemed to be to live in an old farmhouse and work hard to make their own living from the earth they loved. They wanted to stay as far as possible from cities and families, for these represented philosophical concepts they had rejected. To these young people, struggle for money and position was meaningless; they wanted to be free to discover themselves. They were not hostile or aggressive. They did not criticize their parents; rather they pitied them for working so hard and discovering so little of what life was really about. But each in his own way had the feeling that his quest for freedom might be illusory, for to achieve some of his goals he might have to go back into the system and compromise his personal search.

The possibility of retreat from what they had discovered raised another question of great importance to youth, that of values. Many youths today see the impact of technology on life as depersonalizing and demoralizing. Yet their basic concern is with self-discovery and inner development. To abandon their search for meaning in order to cooperate with the processes of dehumanizing industrialization would inflict deep wounds. So the crises of modern youth tend to show up in a whole series of conflicts.

Shall I struggle to maintain my integrity at whatever cost, or should I work out the best possible compromise to hold to my values and yet have some of the benefits of the affluent culture? Should I hold to the measurements of success that are related to money and status, or should I become a dropout from the system in order to find my own way toward inner success? In a culture that can provide so much leisure and so many ways of enjoying it creatively, should I hold to the puritan ideal that gives meaning to life in proportion to the work that is done? Such are the problems and conflict areas that produce the crises of young people today.

In the past the burdens and privileges of maturity were rather clearly defined. Today the situation has changed. In a society in which more and more people are moving toward sick values where manipulation takes the place of relationship, it becomes basic to discover and relate to those who share a quest for values. This is particularly important in marriage, where mutuality in ideas and values is essential to a good relationship. If one marriage partner seeks a genuine relationship and the other wants or is capable only of manipulation, the marriage will not work.

Recent studies of conditioned response with dogs have indicated that if the opportunity to take adaptive action is frustrated, a state of depression follows. As long as a person is free to struggle in his efforts to make things better for himself and others, he can avoid the emotional defeat of depression. If, however, he feels helpless to effect change, he adapts to failure and becomes nonfunctional. This process of adaptation to political and social failure is apparently at work in many young people.

How can this mood of confusion and depression be changed? Because depression often grows from anger turned in upon oneself, and because inability to function often produces the anger, it seems important that useful channels for constructive action be employed to change depression to creative action. The recent concern for ecology is an example of incentive for action both within the self and in society. This incentive is essential to a healthful commitment to maturity and growth.

The maturity that the young adult would in the normal developmental process acquire is a composite. It includes a healthy attitude toward work. It encompasses an ability to make and keep friends, to have confidence in oneself, to be free from excessive doubt, fear, or guilt, and to accept others without prejudice and with respect. An aspect of maturity is the ability to give and receive love, and to improve one's own lot in life without exploiting others in the process. It is the ability to enjoy a wide variety of life experiences and cope with adversity without undue stress. It accepts the place of truth and open-mindedness and a desire to pass on to others what one has learned. When these attitudes and practices can be incorporated into life, the youth has attained an operational maturity.

As the latency period in later childhood is a time for personality consolidation and for practicing stability, so the period between adolescence and full maturity is a time for stabilizing and consolidating life's gains. But when society makes demands that violate ethical ideals—such as killing innocent people in a war regarded as unconstitutional or participating in the abuse of political power—youth can be seriously compromised. The sensitivity and idealism that are so much a part of youthful thinking may be perverted, and the resultant inner confusion and conflict may create intolerable stress. Perhaps this is one reason why the level of suicidal behavior is so high among the youth of our culture.

Normally, youth is a time of maximum health and vigor, personal and social opportunity, and idealism and commitment. It needs the challenges that will stimulate growth and mature functioning. Failing these incentives, youth may become a time of frustration, inner conflict, and disintegrating purpose. The normal crises of youth may be compounded by rapid change, social discontinuity, and personal frustration. The stress of life may create crises that are beyond easy management.

15

Crises of Marriage

Most of the crises we encounter are with people. The closer the relationship, the more possibility there is for stress and conflict. Any relationship with the intimacy, the intensity, and the responsibilities of marriage is likely to have more than its share of crises.

Usually a marriage relationship calls for a major investment of emotion, as well as the psychological, social, and economic resources of life. Yet—strangely—formal training for this important form of self-investment is largely nonexistent. To become a member of one of the learned professions takes from five to ten years of special study. To become a nurse or pharmacist takes several years. Learning a trade may call for several years of apprenticeship. But "learning marriage" may require little more than proximity, glandular stimulation, some moonlight, and a two-dollar license. To be sure, most people take the matter more seriously, yet the opportunity for formal and careful examination of the potential relationship is severely limited.

Over years of doing marriage counseling it has often amazed me that so many marriages do so well considering how they began. Nearly a third of all marriages in our culture do not survive, yet the record for second marriages is good—indicating that people can and do learn in their married behavior.

Another observation I made while doing marriage counseling was that crises are in fact rarely *caused* by the obvious trouble but rather are *precipitated* by conditions, which in turn trigger unconscious negative responses.

I found that men and women expect different things from marriage. In premarital counseling groups I ran there was continual amazement among group members over the difference between men and women in terms of what each desired from the relationship. Often this was an expression of indirect training in their own families. Many of the women said they married for security, while none of the men gave that reason. During the six years that I kept figures, more than three times as many women as men said they married for love. Twice as many men as women sought companionship in marriage. More than three times as many men sought sexual satisfaction. Apparently, many people marry without making any effort to discern the basic interests and needs of their marriage partner. This leads to crises of communication and shared understanding.

When backgrounds differ, it is important to establish communication, to build bridges of understanding. Frank was a sailor who loved his boat and the sea. He fell in love with Ellen in the midwest. It seemed they had everything in common—a perfect match. Ellen had never been on a sailboat, but she looked forward to sharing this part of his life. They were to spend their honeymoon cruising; but as soon as Ellen stepped on the boat she began to feel ill. She was constantly seasick. Later, after valiant efforts to control her sickness by conditioning and medication, she had to abandon sailing completely. While both were disappointed, they are mature about it. Ellen sees Frank and his friends off on their cruises and is waiting with a feast for them when they return. In recent years Frank has been accompanied by his older son, who loves sailing. What could have been a crisis was managed by adaptation.

Such was not the case with Joyce and Jerry. They met in a junior college and felt they were just right for each other. After marriage Jerry was called into military service and Joyce went home to live on the farm. During brief visits things seemed to be going well, but after Jerry's release from the service and their reunion on a permanent basis there was great dissatisfaction. During his service Jerry had traveled and studied and grown. Joyce, on the other hand, had settled down in the life patterns of a small town to wait for Jerry's return. She had not grown; in fact, she had retrogressed. Jerry was disappointed in Joyce's world of small talk, soap operas, and movie magazines. Joyce was hurt by his rejection. The mood was set for conflict, crisis, and separation.

Often the points of conflict are external matters like money, position, house, recreation, and vacations. But these externals are apt to be the things that can be talked about—while the real problems remain out of reach.

Roger came to me to talk about his wife and his marriage. He said that his wife, Faith, made life impossible. When I tried to define his complaints more precisely, he exploded into generalized assaults saying that everything about her turned him off. The more he tried to explain his displeasure in her, the more generalized were his complaints about her. When I interviewed Faith, she seemed to be a woman of taste, attractive and understanding. She was puzzled by Roger's behavior and the conflict that was destroying their relationship, for she had tried to adapt and adjust to his needs. With time and deeper exploration we found that Roger's mother had trained herself to be a school teacher. Her first year of teaching was a disaster because she could not control the children. In disgrace and failure she then quit teaching, married a man nearly twice her age, and in a short time had four children of her own. Children represented a hazard, a source of failure, and she hated them individually and collectively. Her children grew to maturity with deep scars on their personalities. One became an alcoholic and drank himself to death. Another committed suicide. Another became a recluse. Roger was actually the healthiest of the four, but he saw his wife as his mother. He had blinded himself to all of her fine qualities because unconsciously he saw his mother everywhere. With help and hard work he was able to understand his mother's illness and discover his wife as a person. The crisis here was not so much in his marriage as in his childhood.

Sometimes this inherited attitude is related to a minor aspect of living but can be inflated out of proportion when it is not understood. George was brought up on a farm where time was set by the chores and the weather. He was amiable, good-natured, and carefree. Marjorie, his wife, had been brought up on a college campus where her father was a professor. Their marriage was in trouble because of constant bickering and verbal assaults. They seemed to love each other deeply but could not manage the constant day-to-day conflicts. In counseling they began to realize that nearly all of their tension centered on time. Marjorie wanted everything done on schedule. George felt the important thing was to get things done and not worry about the details of a time schedule. He thought Marjorie unreasonable; she thought him careless and irresponsible. Gradually they were able to see that their different attitudes toward time were the major cause of difficulty. College time was set by a bell schedule that all adhered to. But George had a different and just as valid concept of time. The cows had to be milked, but it was the job to be done and not the ringing of bells that set the schedule. Awareness of time and the opportunity to explore it became the basis for a new understanding of the needed areas for adaptation. Even minor unexplored conditions of existence can create stress and make the constant and intimate relationship of marriage a source of hazard and conflict.

Even absurd things can block communication and lead to discord. Mrs. E. asked her lawyer to help her get a divorce. The lawyer had known the couple for many years and thought them devoted and stable, so he suggested a marriage counselor. When she spoke with the counselor Mrs. E. said she couldn't talk about the cause of her distress. Imagining all sorts of major crises, the counselor patiently and carefully led her to explore the causes for so significant a decision as divorce at her age. She finally said she could no longer endure the constant embarrassment: Her husband picked at his nose constantly. She said he would roll his findings into a little ball between his fingers and then shoot it off in the air. His wife was so mortified that she could no longer tolerate his behavior, but she would never think of speaking to him about it. When confronted by the counselor, Mr. E. denied any such behavior but then started doing the same thing then and there. A nervous habit that he was not even aware of had become a source of marital stress and conflict. By lifting it to the level of consciousness and helpful communication, the problem was resolved. When they can't be talked about, even little things can loom large.

Sometimes problems are related to sex but are not perceived that way. Mary and Fred had a good home and income. They wanted a family but their first child was malformed and died because of a genetic defect. They went to a university hospital, where careful examinations determined that this genetic defect would probably appear with each pregnancy. Fred said the physicians might be wrong and they should try again just to make sure. Mary, who had suffered deep grief at the death of her first child, did not want to bring another deformed child into the world. She felt that artificial insemination from a medically verifiable source would solve the problem. Fred said he would rather adopt a child outright than have another man's child by his own wife. Through counseling it was possible to modify Fred's sexual fantasies and relieve his feelings of inadequacy and jealousy. Only time will tell whether there is a residue of his feeling that could affect his attitude toward his child.

When Mr. and Mrs. B. lost their child through infant crib death, Mr. B. was outraged at his wife. He accused her of neglect and wanted a divorce immediately. Mrs. B. had put the child in his crib after his bath at 9:30 and when she went up to check on him at 11:00 he was dead. She called a physician and ambulance at once, but nothing could be done. She was broken-hearted and deeply injured by her husband's accusations. When their pastor became aware of the family's difficulties, he arranged a conference with the family physician. The doctor explained to the couple that medical science was baffled by the infant crib death syndrome; that there was no known cause and no way of anticipating or preventing such an untimely death. The pastor then explained that anger and rage are often part of the grief response. He led the couple to see that in times of crisis people often strike out at the ones closest to them, and that their sorrow could explain their behavior. With the aid of skilled counselors the couple moved through their tragedy to become wiser and more understanding people with a stronger marriage.

In many marriage crises it at first appears that money is the major cause, for money is often at the center of arguments and accusations. It may be assumed that the husband doesn't make enough money or that the wife is a careless manager or a spendthrift. Yet money may well be the scapegoat on which other troubles are hung. It appeared that the marriage of Mr. and Mrs. D. was breaking up over the constant money crisis. However, in counseling it was discovered that Mrs. D. was in a state of constant resentment against her husband because he never seemed to be concerned about her sexual satisfaction; he seemed selfish and unconcerned about her needs. They were unable to talk constructively about their sexual problems. Mrs. D. found that she could really injure her husband by running up bills faster than he could pay them. Whenever he criticized her, she said that the best was not too good for her and her family. The more he pleaded with her to be careful financially the more satisfaction she found in spending money: She would make a purchase with a small down payment and let him worry about paying the rest. Here the solving of a sexual problem was basic to the economic difficulty that was the more obvious threat to the marriage.

The character of the people involved in the marriage is basic to the resolution of crises that occur. Here we are not thinking in terms of qualitative judgments, good or bad, wise or foolish. Rather we are thinking in terms of the basic ability to experience empathetic feelings, to understand and anticipate the feelings of another and respond to them. As mentioned previously, those suffering from serious character disorders usually make unfortunate marriage partners. Their inability to relate to others in any shared venture makes for frustration and failure where responsiveness and mutuality are essential.

Deep within every normal person is a desire to be known as he really is. Perhaps one of the most important desires of the human heart is to find one other person who is as dear to us as we are to ourselves, whose thoughts resonate to our thoughts, whose body is as precious in every part as our own body, and whose aspirations, hopes, and fears are an extension of our own. This capacity for deep relation to one other person may have its finest realization in marriage. When normal people make the commitment of marriage, it is in part an expression of the desire to bring a significant other person into the closest conceivable relationship of body, mind, and spirit.

With such high hopes the risks are serious, for the self that is made vulnerable by its complete openness may be severely injured. The crises of marriage usually appear at a point where the expectation of complete trust and mutuality has been fractured or is seen to be unfulfilled.

Some of this sense of frustration and failure arises from the romantic assumption that marriage is an *event,* when in truth it must always be a *process.* People are alive and dynamic. Experience constantly modifies our lives; and experience that is shared has an impact on those who share it.

It is important to keep in mind the dynamic and constantly changing concept of personality. Discord in marriage can actually be an opportunity for self-examination and growth. Adjustment may become a new adventure into yet unexplored areas of personal fulfillment. Fantasy in sex may, with work and understanding, become reality, the realization of dreams. Companionship may be developed as new skills and shared interests become a part of life. Compatibility may be an ever-growing exploration of the things that can enrich life. Character may be tested and developed through the struggles and tensions that refine it. Money may become a shared resource to accomplish mutually desired goals. Even the echoes of past tradition and relationships with other people can be built into the fabric of life so that they are creative rather than destructive. Early experiences may become the basis for contrast and appreciation rather than blind judgments. Sibling rivalries of the past may be replaced by mature love and appreciation where acceptance does not have to be struggled for. Children then become a shared joy and responsibility rather than a threat and source of competition. When each person in the family is valued for his own qualities, the possibilities for growth are almost unlimited. Loneliness and love are then not two sides of the same coin but rather dimensions of being. The more deeply we love, the more we can sense the value of solitude and the value of being alone together and together alone.

Marriage certainly produces crises in life and it is true that many people fail to make it work for them. But there are also resources in the relationship that can produce growth to resolve many of the crises. Some of us expect too little of marriage; we fulfill our expectations and are disappointed. And others expect more of marriage than is reasonable—as if it were some form of magic. If we examine our emotional and rational investment in marriage, we may find that it is a resource for life. It may cushion our crises and generate resources for skill in managing stress. Marriage, like life, should be a growing thing, a process that moves us through experiences both good and bad toward a special kind of personal fulfillment we may find nowhere else.

16

Crises of the Middle Years

When our value system is threatened we feel anxiety. This in turn makes us hypersensitive and vulnerable. In middle age many of the things we have always felt to be important are suddenly threatened or open to question.

High priority in our culture is given to health, vigor, beauty, and youth. With the exception of Geritol and aspirin ads, most people selling products are young, vigorous, and beautiful.

When we reach the milestone of our fifth decade, we may sometimes feel that life has passed us by. And we will have some evidence for this. We can no longer play the vigorous games we enjoyed so much in the past. We begin to have aches and pains where we never had them before. We find hills where there were none before.

After forty we are likely to look in the mirror and see lines about the eyes, a sag about the chin, some gray hairs here and there, and some bulges that are clearly not all muscle. We can try to comb the gray away, watch our diet, consider plastic surgery, and fool ourselves and others by wearing more youthful clothes. But we know deep inside that things are not quite what they were a decade earlier. We make some changes willingly; other adaptations are forced upon us.

The message is not only from within. We read that a favorite baseball player has decided to retire at thirty-five with the statement that he might as well face it—his legs won't stand up for him anymore. And a football great pushing forty is put on the sidelines because he just doesn't have it anymore. When the weight of opinion falls so clearly upon those over forty, it is impossible to live as if we didn't know what time it was.

The children who were so important a part of our lives now look at us with disdain and sympathy, and indicate they can do better on their own. They say, "You don't need to take me, just give me the keys and I'll drive myself." The future arrives so quickly.

On the other hand, medical science has learned to control many of the scourges of the middle years so that we can look ahead to another forty or fifty years. But what shall we do with them, and how can we manage the crises that accompany them? And before we get a chance to really tackle the question, we are frequently faced with managing some of our parents' affairs. (Our parents, now in their seventies or eighties and enjoying the benefits of medical advances, are not always appealing symbols of our own future.) While many deadly diseases can be controlled, long retirements, high prices, and the costs of specialized care create problems—which often fall on those in the middle years.

At times it seems to those of middle years that they truly stand in the middle, carrying the weight of dependent youth and the dependent aged on their own, not too stable shoulders. This is the age group that pays the major share of taxes, does a major share of the work, and assumes a major share of the responsibility—yet at the same time it must confront the feelings that accompany reduced energy, strength, and physical resource.

A person in the middle years also has a special brand of insecurity. He sees change taking place so rapidly that his skills become obsolete; it is easier to hire a young man or woman out of college to run the computers than to retool an old brain that has so much to unlearn. So job security becomes a concern. Impersonalized industry often turns its back on those with age and experience. Many men who lose positions in their early forties spend months and even years looking for new ones, only to find that they must make a major change in occupation because their former skill has been phased out.

Each sex has its own particular problems to cope with. Women know they are approaching the time in life when glandular change will inevitably appear with menopause. A variety of old wives' tales make it seem a hazard to be met with courage rather than a blessing that can start a new freer, more balanced phase of life. For women who have never had children, involution is a signal that some roles will never be possible. Meeting in counseling sessions with monks and nuns, I was interested to hear the nuns accuse the priests of making unreasonable demands for sacrifice upon those who chose the celibate life only to realize the full meaning of what they had given up when menopause came their way.

For men, the physical processes of the climacteric are more gradual and less disturbing, yet there may be emotional upheaval. In a culture that gives so much significance to sexual performance, the thought that he is not what he used to be can lead a man to feel inadequate. He may replace actions with words by talking more about sex. He may seek stimulation where he found it unnecessary before. He tends to adjust to these changes with denial and with efforts to avoid confronting their meaning. Yet deep within he knows that his way of life is changing and that things will never again be quite the same.

Both men and women during these years may find that they are driven by inner urges so powerfully emotional that they produce behavior changes. A woman who married a man of Eastern European background lived faithfully as his wife and servant for twenty-five years. Then during the turbulence of involution she had a brief encounter with another man. When her husband discovered this, he summarily threw her out of the house and told her he never wanted to see her again. Separated from her children and her home, she lived in poverty and disgrace, uncertain about what had caused her action. Such emotional imbalance may be in part a response to rapid chemical change within the body, and should be understood for what it is.

Jonathan, in his late forties, had always been stable and dependable. Now he began to be interested in his secretary. He took her to dinner and the theater, showered her with gifts, and seemed to feel that she cared for him. When she told him that she was planning to get married and would have to leave his employ, he was deeply injured. He had misread her attitude as love and this had added interest and meaning to his life. He interpreted her plans for marriage as personal rejection and a major blow to his ego. He did not seem to recover and aged more rapidly during the next few years.

Many people during these middle years are so filled with anxiety and apprehension about the aging process that their personalities change. People who had been open and honest with themselves begin to wear masks and play games. They pretend to have feelings they do not have. They act out attitudes foreign to them. They try to show interest in things that are really boring, just to keep up appearances. When they lose their skills in communication through self-deceit, they invite subtle changes in life. They become less and less authentic as people. They become living denials of themselves as they hide more and more behind the deceptive masks they wear. Such bogus selfhood is poor equipment for facing the demands of life at any stage of existence, especially when significant stress exists and the demands for adaptation are considerable.

The alternative to this massive self-deceit is the development of a growing and stronger personality. C. J. Jung labels this growth stage the second adolescence. In the first adolescence there is a struggle to achieve a personality of one's own, independent and strong. During the second adolescence there is a need to discover meaning significant enough to last all the rest of life. The person has now lived enough of his life to know who he is and test the authenticity of his basic philosophy. As Jung points out, many of the crises of the middle years are essentially spiritual. The person decides whether he will coast into old age on the philosophy he has always had or whether he will grow with a new concept of himself and life that can be a renaissance for him. The answer that emerges here will determine whether the crisis of the middle years is a beginning or an end for personal growth.

The answers that he gives to himself as he approaches this period of critical growth will involve such things as guilt, depression, purpose and meaning, fulfillment or failure—or, as Erikson puts it, generativity or stagnation.

Let us look at the problem of guilt. There can be specific guilt or generalized guilt. Specific guilt deals with real problems in human relations and can usually be resolved by confession, restitution, and forgiveness. But generalized guilt has to do with the existential problem of life. A person reviews the major aspects of his life and tries to assess his success or failure. If he finds success, he may judge himself adversely for paying too much for his success. If he finds failure, he confronts it with self-judgment.

Our guilt feelings may show up in a generalized form in relation to our children. We have set standards and goals for them in our own minds, and we have tried to help them achieve those goals. However, as they approach adulthood they may reject the goals we set and decide to set their own goals and choose their own values. It is possible that this may so threaten us personally that we fail to look objectively at what they are doing. We may feel defeated by seeing them drop out of college, experiment with consciousness, enter into an open marriage, or explore the world on foot; or we might feel that they have passed a valid judgment on our values and our way of life. Most parents in recent years have tried to raise their children with enough freedom to make their own choices, establish their own values, and have the courage to live their own lives. So, rather than feeling that their behavior represents a negative judgment on our way of life, we could assume that they have taken us at our word and felt free to discover their own values. Instead of feeling guilty about the directions they have chosen, we might just as reasonably feel they have paid us a compliment—one that has been paid to no other generation of parents. They accepted the freedom we gave them and acted on it with courage and a truly inventive spirit. While we cannot be sure what the future will hold for their experimentation, we can feel confident in their openness and honesty. They have had the courage to move beyond hypocrisy. We should not feel guilty for that.

Depression is often related to feelings of guilt. When we become angry at ourselves, our constant self-judgments eat away at our confidence. Depression often comes from anger turned inward. It can also come from loss of self-trust and personal mastery. If we feel incompetent about life in general, we may develop feelings of helplessness that become self-feeding. The more helpless we feel we are the more helpless we become, and the more helpless we become the more we verify our inadequacy. To break this cycle, we must begin to act on the basis of our personal value, our belief in ourselves and trust in our role in life. Then we can begin to chip away at the painful feelings of depression.

Positive action can reverse the progressive nature of a state of depression. At the physical level we can exercise the large muscle system until the blood flows freely, purifying itself and stimulating glandular and visceral activity. This restoration of a more healthful function of physical organs aids in restoring intrapsychic balance. At the emotional level we can stop passing destructive judgments upon ourselves and begin to accept the universe and the people in it as if they had a right to be themselves rather than projections of our own way of looking at things. And intellectually we can set some goals for our growth into a new and more adequate philosophy of life that can stimulate our development and our next step into maturity.

The life purposes that sustained us during the first phases of marriage, the initial stages of our career, and our early personal development may have exhausted their potential for incentive and growth. Thus we come to another time of self-examination and consolidation. We may have been too preoccupied with externals, neglecting our own spiritual growth. We need a new set of answers for the basic questions—Who am I and why am I? The answers we gave ourselves in the adolescent years were good enough for, but we have outgrown them.

As we ask the same questions in a new context, we can give ourselves new and more valid answers. We now have experience, we have perspective on life; we have tested our old answers and acquired some wisdom through the years. We must find the courage to ask these questions candidly and come up with honest answers to live by. We may be able to make value judgments now that we were not able to make before.

As we look at the things that appear to be failures, we may discover that they are evidences of a higher set of values. Perhaps we were not ruthless enough to make economic killings at the expense of others. Perhaps we were too sensitive to exercise our greed. Perhaps we refused to do the shady things that could have advanced us in business or politics. Instead of thinking in terms of failure, we would do well to begin to value what we have done and to give ourselves credit for it. In the final analysis, life is not measured by what we have acquired but by how we have grown as people.

Erikson says that the major characteristic of the growth stage of the middle years is generativity. This is not so much in biological terms; it is the ability to turn human energy toward goals that are fulfilling in the life process. This involves a cluster of activities: parenthood, training the next generation, stimulating creativity and altruistic concern. It speaks of a positive view of a future where good things can happen.

The alternative to this creative approach to the future is stagnation, a retreat into superficial human relations and a collapse of values. It is marked by a retreat to old ways of thinking. So there may be voracious reading of nostalgic novels, joining of organizations with the mindset of the middle of the last century, retreating into religious activity centered on an outworn cosmology and psychology, and a general retreat from the opportunities of the f.

Instead, we can use this time for renaissance in life, to organize the skills and abilities, the wisdom and knowledge acquired through the years, to make the future interesting and creative. It can be a time for education, new careers, a retooling of the mind. Instead of little hobbies that are merely adjustments to helplessness, there can be large ventures that test and stretch the limits of personal growth. Then, instead of a quiet and helpless compromise with the process of dying, there will be an affirmation of life and growth.

This brave affirmation of the future will bring a new sense of community with other people who have the courage to live. Some of the growth may take place in groups where basic questions are asked. These people dare to look deep inside; they are able to look at others with a new sense of wonder and appreciation.

A woman I knew lived in horror throughout her forties and fifties because she felt she would fall apart at age sixty. In her sixtieth year she went through a time of emotional and physical collapse—just as she had expected. She pulled her world tight about her and settled down to await her death.

The crises of the middle years are less a result of events than of our own attitudes. We make things happen. Our lives can be rich in experience and stimulating in their creativity, or they can be depleted of meaning. If we realize that life is a process and not just a series of events, we can integrate all of living into a development of personality and experience that moves toward self-realization and self-fulfillment.

Then each stage of life becomes the best for us because we are in it. Then life does not lose its wonder but becomes more wonder-filled as we live. The skills we develop in coping with each new era in our personal history can make the crises the stuff of process, growth, and creativity.

17

Crises of Illness and Disability

Our culture has a paradoxical attitude toward illness and health. While we enjoy the most advanced and prestigious medical establishment in history, our antihealth bias is unmatched.

I recently was invited to speak at the annual meeting of a hospital association in a major city. When I arrived, the people were enjoying a cocktail party. Standing around the room were hundreds of people so interested in health that they raised the major portion of the hospital's budget and gave much time and energy to promoting its facilities. However, when I took the opportunity in my address to point out that their way of life involved a contradiction as far as their loyalty to health was concerned, there arose a mood of resentment.

There was no appreciative applause when I pointed out that the best known way of contracting Berger's disease is to take a sip of alcohol to dilate the capillaries and then a drag of nicotine to contract the capillaries until the tiny blood vessels break down and cease to function. No one cheered when I pointed out that in spite of the repeated warnings of the surgeon general, millions of people were busily engaged in acquiring lung cancer with all of its agonies, while other millions were inflicting upper respiratory, cardiovascular, and tissue-damaging assaults upon their beings. No one seemed pleased when I said that tens of millions of people were damaging their livers and kidneys by ingesting alcohol, and that millions of people faced the dissolving of brain tissue until they suffered from alcohol psychoses. There was no burst of approval when I pointed out that many people, in the name of fastidiousness, were assaulting their glandular systems with deodorants and five-day pads.

After the address an air of coolness reigned. I am sure there will be no request for a return engagement. Quite simply I had had the temerity to assault a taboo health area. I had pointed out that much of our behavior has a schizoid component: We value health and work to destroy it at the same time. And our physicians, who have the greatest knowledge about health, appear to have the highest death rate for their age group among any of the professions.

What lies beneath this conflicting attitude toward our own health? Freud pointed out that within everyone there is a will to live and a will to die, with an implicit conflict between the two. And Freud illustrated his idea by his ubiquitous cigar and his courageous fight against his own cancer. Existentialists would say this conflict arises from our anxiety about death. Our anxiety produces nonrational behavior that actually drives us toward our death.

Our culture is flooded with the evidences of this conflict about sickness and dying. Our irrational behavior indicates the inner conflict. Although we know there are twenty percent more stillborn babies among women who smoke, we somehow do not think that smoking mothers are guilty of murderous behavior. Although, over a ten-year period, sixty-seven Americans died from cigarette smoking for every American who met death in Southeast Asia, we tend to think that the war was a major catastrophe while cigarette smoking is an acceptable form of social behavior. When death anxiety is so prevalent that we blot out our awareness of hazards, we become impotent to deal with nonrational behavior.

In fact, in our culture, we even go to the other extreme. We actually reward illness and nonrational behavior and penalize those who maintain health and who act with clear perception of cause-effect relationships. Let us illustrate. When do people get special consideration—flowers from friends, notes and gifts, breakfast in bed, sick leave, and insurance benefits? Not when they are well, to be sure. No, people who are ill—and this illness may often be psychogenic—get special consideration and love. They are fussed over and rewarded for their weakness. Those who remain well are given extra work and expected to increase their love-giving and burden-carrying. Increased assignments and responsibility go to the healthy to make up for those who seek the benefits of escape into illness.

But being ill is not all irrational or all beneficial. Illness comes from four general sources: (1) The conflict of the organism with the environment. This is implicit in fungus growth, viral infection, or invasion of the organism by wounds or injuries. (2) The basic strength of the organism, inherited or otherwise, which resists breakdowns in functioning or succumbs to stress. (3) The effect of accidents of one type or another. (4) The psychological attitude, which bears on every other form of organic function. These four conditions can bring their own form of crisis, for we are closely bound up with the physical dimension of our being.

Catastrophic illness always brings some aspects of life into question. Pain can so affect a person that his views of himself and others go through major changes. He may become resigned and build up tolerance to pain, or he may become so self-centered that he becomes a tyrant who manipulates others for his own comfort.

A person who enters a hospital often suffers an identity crisis. But the hospital experience also raises certain questions about life and death that we might ordinarily avoid asking. If a person is ill enough to be hospitalized, he may be sick enough to die. How will we confront the possibility of our non-being? Will we panic, reducing our emotional strength and so retarding the process of recovery? Or will we bring into action new and unused resources that can move us toward health and wholeness? The answers here are subjective forces that we organize to cope with the crisis of ill health. The distinction between anxiety and fear is important, for anxiety can produce disorganization and life-destroying action while fear can bring into focus the energies needed for restoration of wholeness.

Our culture tends to be death-denying and death-defying. That means that we regard the possibility of death as remote from us. This is reinforced in us in a variety of ways. It is permissible to show dead Southeast Asians in newsfilm, but not dead Americans. Numerical magic is used to show that for every American casualty there are forty or fifty people of other colors and nationalities who meet death. We emphasize the presence of a small number of prisoners of war and look away from the large number of casualties who will never return. We may play with illusory death in entertainment and avoid confronting real death. None of this, however, is enough to allay our anxiety about our mortality. It merely makes it more difficult to deal honestly and openly with the reality that we must all encounter.

Major forms of disability, which tend to reduce life, produce a set of crises that may be more chronic in nature. Blindness, with the closing out of a large segment of life experience, often calls for a reordering of personal experience and values. The crippling effect of multiple sclerosis, which makes a person immobile and largely nonfunctional, can disrupt the life of the individual who has the disease as well as those around him. With this and similar diseases, such as arthritis, new skill may be developed for managing the circumstances. However, this may be accompanied by a new type of self-centeredness and tyranny over others that can actually destroy human relationships and breed unending hardships.

War casualties bring special crises. The marred and disfigured bodies may harbor souls filled with resentment. Surviving family members may face conflicts in their desire to forget and their inability to do so. Those who are so physically destroyed that they cannot relate to others produce an unending and chronic grief, for the work of mourning cannot really be done. So the emotional crisis, with all its heartache and frustration, is projected indefinitely into the future. How can those close to such a person—as to the mentally ill or the retarded—plan a future, remarry, or find release from frustration when the cruel facts of life keep restating themselves in every waking hour and in troubled dreams?

As medical skills for saving lives improve, the number of people who suffer from lingering and chronic ailments grows. Instead of preventing death, it seems that heroic medical intervention often prolongs the process of dying. So the aged live on long after their minds have ceased to function normally. The wounded and the damaged survive for years after they have been separated from normal relationships.

What can be done about these crises of illness and disability?

Perhaps the first thing we need to do is develop a new working definition of life and death. For so long we have thought of death as the moment when the heart ceases to function. Yet when we see death as a process we gain a different perspective. We can see the long slow process of deterioration toward the inevitable biological conclusion. We can adjust to death gradually, recognizing that the person we had known is slowly becoming a remnant or echo of the person who once was.

Medically, a careful redefinition of death is taking place. I sat for a week with a group of lawyers and physicians who were trying to reexamine the nature of life and death. They considered the problem of when life begins—so important in the emotional problems related to abortion. They considered the problem of when death occurs—from social and psychological viewpoints, as well as biological. Is it when the heart ceases to beat, or when the flow of oxygen to the brain ceases, or when meaningful capacity for communication and relationship ends? The case of Mrs. Wrigley is often referred to in considering this problem. Her organic functions were maintained for more than ten years after any form of consciousness was observed. Did she die when the complicated processes of medical intervention finally failed to maintain organic activity? Or did she die a long time earlier? In fact, most people begin to withdraw the emotional capital they have invested in another when there appears to be no sign of "meaningful" life. If we think of life as the structure of relationships that give meaning to our existence, we may feel death occurs when life loses its meaning for the one who is dying. While this may not be a legal or a medical definition, it will serve the person experiencing the loss. He may gradually accept the changes that come with dying without waiting for a final heartbeat.

Also, we can recognize that there is a psychic component in all illness. Sometimes this psychic element is so strong that it can be activated to restore life. Many people apparently die because they have been isolated from meaningful life and relationships. The conspiracy of deceit and silence that isolates so many critically ill persons may stimulate the depression. This depression will reduce vital functioning and so hasten organic deterioration. The converse, confronting the physical condition openly and honestly, may stimulate emotional responses that affect the body chemistry and aid in the process of restoration. All the resources needed to produce this restoration are already within the person. However, it may well be that they await stimulation by some other force at work in life. In some instances, psychic or spiritual healing appears to be an agent for stimulating this release of healing energy in the ill person. At other times the agency may be the power of suggestion, the intervention of an authoritative person (such as a physician), or some hope that can be stimulated by the prospect of important medical intervention.

A third factor that may work to restore the healing energy in an ill person is the capacity for meaningful communication with others. This may work for both the ill person and those who are coping with the dying process of a relative or friend.

The spirit of denial so prevalent in dying makes it difficult to move with the process. Instead, deception and fractured communication surround the people involved until the final biological event is upon them. Denying themselves the opportunity to approach the crisis in easy stages, they plummet into the terminal event.

A fourth approach is being developed now. Professional

groups are working with the dying patient and his family. Recognizing the intensity of the crisis and the impact it may have on those engaged in it, these people are working for a climate of confrontation. Nurses are trained to let people talk out their feelings. Physicians are paying attention to the special needs of families. Clergymen and social workers are recognizing the importance of special care for those in grief. Scientific research has established that patients and families who keep open the channels of honest communication move through their crises with less traumatic impact. In fact, it has been found that pain can be reduced by communication, while the denial of communication produces anxiety and the anxiety produces physical tension. The tension pulls at the muscle structure, causing spasticity or tearing at lesions. This intensifies the pain. But if the anxiety is released through healthful communication, the spasticity and tension are reduced and with them the pain.

With a chronic disability, where the impact on normal family living is constant, we are learning that the rights of those who are normal and healthy should not be jeopardized. Special treatment and custodial facilities make it possible for the disabled to have care in a setting responsive to their special needs. At the same time the rest of the family is allowed to pursue its activities of growth and development. The concept of loyalty, which imposes the affliction on many, is now seen to be counterproductive.

Deep in the religious thinking of some people is the idea that illness is related to punishment. This unhealthy form of religion seems to think that the devastation of life is a warranted response for human failure. It is more productive to realize that illness can come from many causes and that the wisest procedure is one that best meets the needs of the ill and disabled on the one hand, and offers opportunities for healthful growth and development for all on the other.

Only in recent decades has the importance of emotional factors in illness been emphasized. It may well be that our attitude toward illness can be modified so that we do not invite or reward it. Perhaps we can fit the nature of illness into a larger pattern, recognizing the cause-and-effect factors so clearly that guilt and punishment will be separate from illness and disability. Then wise and responsible behavior in relation to health will become a guide. The healthful will be rewarded and the diseased treated in mind and body to restore them to true wholeness of being.

18

Crises of the Aging and the Aged

As modern medicine works to preserve life, new problems are created for those who are preserved. A century ago there were two and a half million persons over sixty-five in our country. By the turn of the century it is estimated there will be more than thirty million. We have learned how to make millions of older people, but we have not learned how to make life rich and full for them.

We call them senior citizens, mature Americans, the aging, the aged, the old folks. We joke about them, saying you can tell them by the four Bs—bridges, bald spots, bifocals, and bulges. Yet we are uneasy about the fact that many of these older people seem to be misfits. They are the uncomfortable legacy of scientific advancement. They have outgrown the society that has created them, and their role is confused for them and confusing for most everyone else. We try to organize them into social groups, recreational groups, or political power groups, but find that they are not easily organized.

During a few weeks I spent in Japan recently I had a chance to observe the place of older people in an Oriental culture. Here the aged were considered wise and were treated with respect and high regard. In the private shrines the aged were the leaders of worship and their role was defined by the ancient precept,

"Filial piety is what distinguishes men from birds and beasts."

Such attitudes were once valued in our American tradition, but changes have come about. What has happened in our culture to change the role and status of the older members of society? Changes in architecture, lifestyle, and economic interests have not provided a place of importance for the older person. This was not done so much by design apparently as by the unplanned movement away from a consideration of their needs and resources. Although social security provides some minimal economic support, it hardly represents a comfortable way of life. Elderly parents can be a financial burden on their children. Illness may quickly use up life savings. We manage to modify some forms of social segregation, yet we create another as we move older people into retirement centers and rest homes. For the large segment of our society that is aged or aging, we have not really created the good life. These people who have so much to offer are treated as if they are no longer significant.

Old age should be a time for integration of the whole life experience, for fulfillment. Yet for so many it becomes a time of self-disgust and despair. The disgust comes from no longer being able to produce and be useful. This is the old puritan ethic that equates useful life without useful work. When people cannot make their bodies work for socially valid tasks, they turn against their bodies with disdain. The despair is a form of chronic depression that is acted out in a high rate of suicide among those over sixty-five—some figures show a suicide rate *five times* that of persons in the middle years. Death lurks as an ever-present possibility for the aged. There is fear of the loss of personal dignity and direction of one's destiny that may occur with lingering illness. With this fear, it becomes tempting to try to control death.

Retirement often causes a crisis of confidence. If a person has done useful work and enjoyed doing it, he may feel he has experienced a form of death when he retires. The crisis is frequently compounded by a downward change in economic status, which may spell an end to long-standing interests and enjoyments. There may be a loss of abilities along with the loss of opportunity to develop them. In effect a person is having to confront aspects of his dying without the benefit of being dead. The existence he is compelled to continue may well be a hollow echo of his earlier life.

The crisis of confidence that accompanies retirement may move in two directions: withdrawal and personal growth.

Older people often feel resentful of the young and may accuse them of neglect or a withering away of values. They may retreat from life, rejecting social contacts that were formerly important to them. They may take a hypercritical attitude toward other people: Everyone else is stupid and the world is a mess so we may as well withdraw from it as much as possible. This is one form of defense of the threatened ego; when it cannot function with self-confidence, it can at least try to downgrade all other ego competition.

On the other hand, the crisis of confidence can release new resources for self-discovery and personal growth. Retirement provides a time for release from stress, where a person is able to take a relaxed stance toward life. In his relaxed mood he may find it possible to refine his interests, discover new ones, and employ new resources. Instead of having life collapse about him, he will not only stay alive but also gain new satisfactions from living.

We know that it is possible for people to stay active and creative well into their ninth or tenth decade. Casals, Toscanini, and Picasso are evidence of this fact. Apparently it is the stimulus of interest in our lives that preserves the creative function.

There are three different types of aging at work. One, the *chronological,* is measured by the calendar but may be vetoed to some extent by personal action; just because so much time has elapsed since birth does not mean we must live in a particular way. *Biological* time has its own mechanism for measurement; some people have old bodies at thirty while others are youthful and vigorous at seventy. *Psychological* time is measured by yet another set of standards, and the attitude a person has toward his own aging may hasten or postpone his deterioration. If a person makes friends with the aging process, it can be friendly to him. If he resents and fights aging, it may well fight back and he will be the loser.

Usually there are built-in mechanisms that help a person accept the aging process. The wisdom that comes with long experience can help him to use his energy more carefully to do the things that are important. The profligacy of youth is left far behind.

Life is sustained by relationship. It grows through shared experience and constant exploration. When loneliness is allowed to settle in on life there will be an atrophy of being. The stimulation of shared living is lost; instead, one relives the past in lonely reveries. For many who have lost a life partner, a new marriage will provide new experience, companionship, and a look toward the future rather than immersion in the past, which can no longer enrich life.

A study done at Princeton University shows that humans reach a peak of creativity at about thirty-five years of age. Then creative ability begins to fall away. At the physical level there is a steady decline. However, at the emotional level the high degree of effective investment may persist with little or no deterioration for decades, and at the intellectual level—where the stimulus is adequate—the effective mental output may show little decline well into the eighth decade. It has also been discovered that the condition of senile dementia can actually be reversed by a renewal of interest in life. Companionship, communication, and a stimulating atmosphere bring back the mental energy that banks the fires of life so that they glow again with new heat.

I once received a request from a family to help protect an old lady from herself. When the family left for work she became irresponsible, leaving open the door of the refrigerator, burning the bottom out of tea kettles, and failing to close doors in winter. It seemed like a case of senile deterioration. So I took her to the county hospital for a checkup. Two weeks later the director of the hospital called me and said, "You can pick up your old lady any time today." In response to my query he replied that she appeared to be perfectly normal—as soon as they got the alcohol out of her system. When I talked with the old lady she said that she had never taken a drink until two years before. She heard on television that it made people feel better, so she decided to try it. While the rest of the family was out she went to a nearby store and bought her bottles. When she was finished with them she carefully placed them in the garbage containers of neighbors down the street. In no time at all she had substituted another problem for her loneliness and had become nonfunctional. When she was placed in a retirement home with other people her own age and new interests, she took on new life and functioned well for several years. This particular form of self-applied psychotherapy may be more widespread than we assume. In our culture it is accepted practice to relieve stress by modifying consciousness. It is no wonder that some of our older people try it.

Another critical area for the older person is the gradual buildup of suspicion of others, to a state of paranoia. This is usually another manifestation of the mood of disgust and despair. Feelings of guilt about nonproductive living are projected outward upon other people. It is then an easy step to thinking that other people have hostile feelings against them, or even to the assumption that the hostility will be implemented in direct action. So older people may make telephone calls to neighbors or relatives or even the police claiming that they are being poisoned. These charges are often difficult for those closest to them to accept, and the stresses involved in trying to manage the older person may become even greater. The pain of suspicion is extended outward to complicate the lives of all who share the family relationship.

Often the aging process brings suffering. No matter how gently the aged person is treated, every movement may bring sharp pain. Every trip to the bathroom or every meal may involve distress. Life is reduced to an anguished round of caring for elemental needs. Sedation may relieve some of the pain but it also reduces the awareness of life and its benefits. Within the context of family living the care of the painridden person may complicate life so much that all living is reduced to the basic needs of the sufferer. When specialized care is considered, the sufferer may feel rejected and abandoned by those close to him. Even attempted solutions to the problem can create problems.

With such a complicated problem, what can be said and done about the aging process that is positive and useful? Where the individual is not severely ill physically, there are so many ways to make aging a rewarding experience. I have found that students who are having difficulty with their parents have a deep need to share their lives with some older person. This may be a deeply imbedded psychic need. It may be an effort to establish continuity of human experience. The grandfather figure in life and literature is well established. It may be that in our culture, with its rapid change and built-in discontinuity, there is a greater need than ever before for the person who can listen, understand, and accept the youth who is venturing into life. Through the rediscovery of the grandparent role we may be reestablishing veneration of the aged and their wisdom.

The period of retirement may also be a time for doing important unfinished business of living. In our acquisitive culture many people have been obsessed with acquiring goods they know they cannot take with them. If they have a great investment in things that are earthbound, they make the grief in anticipating their own death more acute. Perhaps they could find a satisfaction in giving away what they possess to those they know will appreciate it. They could thus gain a personal satisfaction, while also reducing their own potential grief at losing their possessions. I have tried this, and it worked for me.

For years I collected first editions of books by famous authors, autographed if possible. Many of the two hundred and fifty books I had collected never came off the shelves from year to year. A few years ago I decided to start giving them away. At Christmas time I would select a few copies and send them to people I knew would enjoy and value them. The response has been so personally satisfying that now I do not wait for special days for my private giveaway. If I discover that someone I know has a great interest in Jonathan Edwards or William James, I surprise him with a rare first edition. This special way of making others happy may be one of the richest rewards of the older years. And its special byproduct is that while it reduces the number of things you can't take with you, it also brings the joy of giving and receiving into your life.

Sometimes the unfinished business of living is found where least expected. A physician told me of two elderly hypochondriacs who pestered him endlessly until he had run out of ideas. In desperation he prescribed that they learn Spanish. So they started studying it, practiced it together, began reading Spanish literature, decided to visit Mexico and South America. They became so absorbed in their new life that they forgot their aches and pains. They thanked the harried doctor for opening up a new world for them.

The unfinished business of living can open doors of satisfaction and recognition. It can change boredom to new life. Grandma Moses had no interest in painting until she had completed most of the tasks of her normal life span. Then she found a new world and she loved it.

The older years make it possible to experience a different kind of love. During the earlier years love is always a mixture of privilege and responsibility. With the aged love can be free from many of the responsibilities of the past; it can be sheer enjoyment of others. The onset of love in the early years has been characterized as a first fine careless rapture. With the older person it may well be a last fine careless rapture—one that enriches human relationships.

The older years may also be a time for bringing wonder and beauty back into life. The idealism of adolescence has probably been lost in the demands for making a living and doing those other things that are so much a part of the busy years. Now it may be time to dust off the ideals and rediscover the beauty, wonder, mystery, and truthfulness of existence. The chance to stand before a great painting, to read a great book, to enjoy some great music may have been long postponed. But it need be put off no longer. With a new age of appreciation, the rewards of life may be openly enjoyed. This investment in spiritual growth calls for little energy and strength, but it will fill the older years with beauty and will nourish the soul.

When life is filled with wonder and beauty, the hazards of existence recede. Life is strengthened, so there is less need to fear death. And when we reduce fear of death we discover a new wonder in life. The older years can produce the spiritual fulfillment that becomes the crowning experience of life. The person who experiences this sense of spiritual fulfillment directs it outward, so that instead of being part of the problem of aging he becomes part of the solution to the problem. The future belongs to those who are ready for it.

19

Let Yourself Be Helped

Up to this point we have concentrated on the general nature of crises and on understanding the specifics of crises as they affect different ages and conditions. It will now be our task to discover what we personally can do about the crises that occur in our lives, to see what we can do to manage them more wisely.

Professionals who care for people in crises often complain that people wait too long to call in professional help and so make the problem more difficult. What keeps people from seeking help as soon as possible? What keeps them from foreseeing problems in their germinating stages? What is the fear that holds them back?

What is the first thing we do in an emergency? Usually we make our own nonprofessional diagnosis. This is a necessity: We must decide whether we can manage alone or whether we need help.

If we have a legal problem, we decide whether we wish to make a simple plea or seek the guidance of a lawyer and fight the matter through the courts. If we have a toothache, we decide either to wait for it to go away or to seek the skill of a dentist. If our youngster is ill, we decide whether it is serious enough to call a doctor or whether it will clear up with a good night's sleep. We make practical decisions of this nature all the time. If by using our own nonprofessional judgment we make the wrong decision, we may arrive too late with too little.

The following amusing case may illustrate the dangers of self-diagnosis. Jane was an intelligent, healthy, and emotionally well-balanced young woman. She had a good position as a teacher, had been married five years, and had seldom missed a day of work because of illness. When she began to have dizzy spells on arising in the morning, she was disturbed but not alarmed. She did not even mention it to her husband but decided she must suffer from eye strain and might need glasses. She stopped in at the office of an ophthalmologist, who examined her and said that her eyes were in excellent condition. Then she remembered reading that sometimes dizziness accompanies heart weakness, so she made an appointment with a heart specialist who found her heart in fine condition. Now she was a bit anxious. She had heard that sometimes these symptoms are a sign of emotional disturbance, so she made an appointment with a neuropsychiatrist. He found no evidence of abnormality in her emotions or her nervous system. In distress she blurted out her anxiety to her husband, who was not as inventive as she was. He called the family physician, who gave Jane a thorough physical examination, suggested that she get plenty of rest, eat wholesome food, and not worry about anything except her regular monthly visit to him, for in about eight months her symptoms would be replaced by a son or daughter.

In a time of crisis it is important to put ourselves in the care of someone who can look at all there is of us rather than try to diagnose our own condition and delay the treatment we may need.

The first thing to do in a crisis is to manage ourselves—our fears, our uncertainties, and our apprehension—in order to remain alert to warning signals that may indicate a change in our physical condition.

We must beware of false pride. If the problem is not physical we may be so embarrassed that we hold back from admitting its existence to anyone else—until it goes out of control and forces itself on us and those around us.

Many people have a basic distrust of others and their intentions, so they may separate themselves from the help they need just when it could be most useful. This distrust can apply to professional help, too—and this is dangerous. What lies behind our inability to gauge our own needs and the resources available to us?

Ironically, our increased knowledge is a contributor to our dilemma. A recent study of physicians as patients may illuminate this question. It might be assumed that physicians, who know more about the problems of illness and health than others in our culture, would make the best patients. We would expect them to be most able to understand what was being done and to cooperate. This does not appear to be the case. The study shows that their knowledge got in the way of their cooperation —because of their understanding and their emotional involvement with it. They built a conflict between their objective judgments and their subjective needs. The same knowledge that was so useful in working with others could become a handicap when they were the patients.

Ours is the most medically sophisticated era in history. More people are reading articles about medical research, problems of disease, and methods of treatment than ever before. People are deeply interested in their bodies and their functioning. As a result, we may think we know more than we really do—and this may stand in the way of our fullest cooperation with the professional.

However, if this greater knowledge of the healing arts among the general public is used in its proper context, it can stimulate a wiser response. When the importance of early care is emphasized, the process of seeking health care will start earlier and be most beneficial.

Some of the hesitancy to seek early treatment is due to certain reasonable fears people have about health authorities. They may, based on past experience, rightfully fear a kind of dictatorial attitude. Those who deliver health care usually insist on doing it where they choose, when they choose, and how they choose. A conflict may arise when an individual wants to have some say in decisions about his own health care.

In general the physician is the leader of the health care team. And usually the hospital is the best equipped and most convenient place for the delivery of health care. There is an implicit understanding, then, that people are to adapt to the services— rather than the services to people. Plans for medical service are clearly set up *for* people and not *with* them. There is an apparent assumption that the aims of science and the aims of people are not the same. In order that people may become more responsive to their health needs, all these assumptions will have to be reexamined. Instead of inviting resistance, we should be eliciting cooperation. The care of the body cannot easily be separated from all other aspects of personality. Once we accept this fact and begin to act on it, we will have taken a big step toward improving health care.

Part of the process of getting help is purely mechanical. Just exactly how do you get started?

One of the first things you should do when you move into a new community is to make a careful list of all the resources available there. Then, if you encounter any difficulties, you will have your list right there to consult.

Some services, such as the fire department and the police department, are easy to locate because of their emergency nature. These two particularly should be noted accurately, for the lines of authority are often confusing, especially in the suburbs. In emergencies it is important to be able to save time by doing the right thing at once.

But the less dramatic emergencies may end by causing us more difficulty—for when we don't know what to do we often do nothing for a while and this may be valuable time lost. So let us now consider how to find resources in our communities and use them appropriately. The types of crises that can arise are so great in number and range that we will limit our exploration to methods and not to an inclusive detailing of all the resources available.

Johnny is in the second grade. He comes home from school,

apparently bubbling over with enthusiasm. When he talks he begins to stutter. Is his stuttering something that needs to be cared for at once or is it something he will outgrow? Is it a physical problem or is it emotional? What can be done to avoid the handicap in communication that would come with an unresolved stuttering problem? These are the questions that immediately come to the mind of Johnny's mother, who must confront his problem with him.

Johnny's mother should not be expected to be an authority on such a health care problem. But she should be concerned enough about it to begin doing something constructive. She should know at once that punishment would serve no useful purpose. Drawing attention to the problem or laughing about it also would not be helpful. She should know that it is a symptom and so she should seek *guidance* on the meaning of the symptom. If there is a child guidance clinic in the community she could look there. She might find out, through the clinic's testing resources, that Johnny's stuttering is a temporary matter that is due to his knowledge advancing more rapidly than his articulation skills. Or she might find out that it is a manifestation of his emotional stress in a threatening environment; here treatment may mean help in handling the stress. In either case, Johnny's problem is kept in focus.

If there is no child guidance center, there may be a school psychologist or a pediatrician who would have knowledge of what is involved in Johnny's behavior. In rural areas none of these services may be easily accessible; in this event, the wealth of material provided by the federal government may be useful. Special bulletins of great worth and low cost have been prepared by experts to help with the management of nearly every handicap a child may develop. These bulletins cover speech problems, sight problems, hearing problems, and a whole variety of other physical conditions. You can get them by writing to your representative in Congress or by a direct request to the child care division of the Department of Labor. Local libraries also may have books or pamphlets that can give insight into the management of the problem and list available resources. The fact is, if you explore the matter with care, there are usually ways of meeting the problem wisely.

With health problems the starting point should be the family physician. From here, the process can move out toward specialized resources. For nearly every major disease there is a national committee that provides technical advice and even, in many instances, financial assistance.

Many problems that involve health care also have a significant psychological or mental health dimension. If you discover that your teenage children are experimenting with any of the hazardous drugs, intervention is needed for their personal and social health. As a national problem it has drawn major attention as well as treatment resources and financial aid for the treatment process. If you suspect that someone in your family is an alcoholic, there are usually state and local agencies that can help. Getting started is as simple as making a phone call and setting up an appointment.

If a member of your family or someone you know seems depressed, easily angered, highly suspicious, or suffers from dizziness or blackouts, the problems may be physical or mental. Nonrational behavior and disturbed functioning may have a physical cause, as with a brain tumor. Or they may be related to emotional stress. In either instance the need is for skilled diagnosis. Here too the starting point is usually the family physician, who can make the necessary referrals for further testing and treatment.

Many of the crises that occur will not be related to any physical or mental problem. With children, they may be behavior problems; with adults, marriage problems. Since these problems can cause suffering and disruption of life, it is important to move toward their treatment as quickly as possible. Here the child psychologist or the social agency that supervises child therapy may be the resource; the marriage counselor or the pastoral counselor may have the specialized training for confronting and working through the life-disturbing marital conflict.

If there is an explosive form of anger or destructive behavior, the police may be the first resource, followed by admission on an emergency basis to a hospital or treatment center.

Sometimes the problems are moral, social, or spiritual. They may involve infidelity, community prejudice, or excessive guilt. Here help may come from the marriage counselor, the human rights agency, or the clergyman. The best way to confront the problem is to be completely honest with yourself and with the person to whom you turn for professional help. Deceit and games just delay the process and threaten the therapeutic relationship.

Many communities have resources for preventive care, as well as therapeutic intervention when problems become more acute. The local mental health agency or social work agency may have conferences that pinpoint early manifestations of potentially critical situations so that corrective action can be taken when it may be most beneficial.

Perhaps one of the major causes for delay in seeking help with family crises is economic. People have learned that professional services are costly. They may wait as long as they dare before calling for help. This may, in the long run, prove economically unsound. The delay may make the problem more difficult to manage and may result in far greater expense.

People in need are unaware of many of the resources for economic aid. Most social agencies have a clinical fee scale based on income and ability to pay. Many professionals provide their skills under public defender or clinical arrangements so that the same resources are available through a need scale arrangement. Even in private practice, special considerations are often granted on request. In most communities, when the situation warrants, there are funds and services that can be made available at community cost. This is especially true for widows, dependent children, and those qualified for old age assistance.

Most communities have various funds to provide help in meeting crises. Often these funds are little publicized. They may be endowed funds entrusted to a church for management or endowed beds in hospitals awaiting assignment to those who qualify. They may be discretionary funds supervised by pastors or trust funds administered by lawyers. Often there are national endowments or foundation funds available for those who qualify. Where there is special need it is important to search out the financial help that may be accessible. These funds can usually be discovered by the social service departments of hospitals or social workers in community agencies.

Too often people with crises retreat into their pride and isolate themselves from the help that may be awaiting them. It is important to put yourself in the mood to accept help and then move toward the resources available. This may take some imagination and energy, but the fruits will usually be worth the effort. This effort may also open doors of relationship and service in the community that will be useful to you and others in the future. For the more wisely we learn to manage each crisis as it comes, the more skill we will have for meeting the future crises that are an inevitable part of the life experience of all of us.

20

The Therapy of Acting Out

Acting out means putting our emotional impulses into action. Many of the things we do are the acting out of our inner crises. Some of these things are destructive and some are healthful and creative. When the impulses emerge from troubled or unhealthy conditions of mind and emotion, the activity is often socially threatening. We have seen much of this in recent years: prejudice and deeply disturbed emotional states breaking through in acts of assassination and abuse of political power.

Unhealthy acting out is often self-destructive in nature. An example of this is the person who overeats when he feels rejected, or overdrinks to ease an inner discomfort.

Our dreams are the acting out, at the lower levels of consciousness, of the feelings we work to repress consciously. These feelings exist in all of us but are usually not expressed directly. Often they show up in disguised form in dreams or other forms of behavior. A person who commits murder is acting out, in explosive form, the hostility that floods his emotions. When psychosis takes over a person's functioning, it is usually the acting out of an emotional state that cannot be managed within normal bounds.

But the processes of acting out need not be destructive; in fact, they may be highly therapeutic. In this chapter we will center on these more positive forms of acting out. We will explore how they may become valid resources for helping us to cope with emotional and social crises.

Anthropologists have discovered that all societies with a high level of group organization have as a part of their cultural heritage a wide variety of processes for acting out deep feelings. These acting out processes are called rites, rituals, and ceremonies. The more primitive the acting out procedures, the more primitive is the society. When a culture has developed complicated, significant, and socially meaningful ceremonial activity, it is usually a highly developed society.

In studying this, anthropologists have observed that most ceremonial activity clusters about the common life crises. Obviously, then, one social function of the ceremonies is to help people cope with the crises that are so much a part of human experience.

The rites, rituals, and ceremonies range from simple and everyday events like saying hello to highly specialized activities involving preservation of a national tradition or transfer of political power.

Let us look at the nature of some of these acting out rituals. Life is so filled with them that we may not even realize what they are. Ritual is so basic to our communication of emotions that we may take it completely for granted and not bother to look more closely.

As I walk down the street, I see a friend coming toward me, holding out a cigar and smiling. I immediately draw certain conclusions based on his behavior. He knows that I do not smoke and I know that he does not smoke, so his act of offering me a cigar must have another and symbolic meaning. I proceed on that assumption and offer congratulations. He fills me in on gender, time of arrival, and the condition of his wife. Then he happily proceeds on down the street with his supply of phallic symbols and a big smile.

In this set of circumstances, we were both acting out through symbolic behavior. Becoming a parent is a big event in life.

There is a need and desire to communicate about it, but it is not considered proper for a man to brag about his biological prowess. A rooster may crow loudly whenever a hen lays an egg; this is approved behavior in the barnyard. But with humans there is a need for some other procedure for expressing deep feelings. So the acting out centers on a clearly recognizable symbol, in this case a cigar. This immediately sets off a ritualized exchange of information which serves as communication of our feelings.

Ritualized behavior often occurs on a grand scale. The university I attended has a large sports arena called The Bowl. Each fall a number of events take place there that would be considered nonrational if they were examined from a purely logical point of view. Tens of thousands of people travel millions of miles collectively for these events. Together they spend well over a million dollars for tickets, travel, hotel accommodations, new clothes, and antifreeze in order to sit and shiver in the fall chill for a couple of hours and watch eleven athletes from another center of higher learning engage in physical combat to establish the superiority of their university. The device used to establish which university is superior is the moving about on a grass field of a piece of inflated animal hide. If a visitor from Mars were to land in the middle of the screaming crowd at the Yale Bowl on a Saturday afternoon in late November, he might be inclined to activate his retrorockets at once and explain to his control center that the earth was the insane asylum of the universe. But we who attend the game do not judge ourselves thus, for we know the symbolic meaning of the event. We know the emotional stimulus of institutional loyalty. We know the satisfaction of meeting old friends and enjoying a festive occasion. The significance of ritualized behavior is the meaning attached to it by those who participate in it. It is a language all its own with powerful emotional meaning.

This kind of group behavior centers on life crises and emotional states. Birth, the onset of adolescence, the creating of a family, the death of an individual all have critical possibilities —all are emotionally charged events with crisis implicit in them. In broader terms, society has its special ceremonial occasions. In politics we have inaugurations. In tradition we have holidays, museums, and anniversary celebrations. In religion we have ordinations. In education there are graduations.

In all of these events there is a combination of emotional meaning with nonrational behavior. For instance, at graduation it would be much simpler to send each graduate his diploma through the mail and be done with it. Yet we plan ahead for an elaborate series of events employing unique attire, solemn parades (which are really stately dances), special music, and ceremonial acting out that is stately as well as expensive. Why all the fuss? Largely because there is a dimension of meaning that can be expressed in this form of acting out but cannot be achieved without it.

When a couple gets married it would be much simpler to go to the justice of the peace and make the contract legal, but most people don't do it that way. Instead, they plan ahead to make the moment of public commitment as special and as sacred as possible. Special attire that will probably be worn only once, a special group of people who will probably be brought together only once, special music, special food, special flowers, and everything else that can be made special for the occasion is employed. The money spent for the events surrounding a ten or fifteen minute service could be used to make a down payment on a new home. But it is considered valid and appropriate for this important and potentially critical commitment in life to be surrounded with as much affirmation and public confirmation as possible.

When someone dies, it would be easy to take the wornout body and dispose of it quickly and without ceremony. But in most cultures the body is carefully prepared for its burial or cremation and becomes the center for a whole variety of ceremonies. In fact, the degree of advancement of a civilization appears to be related to the degree of respect shown for the dead body. These ceremonies give a chance for acting out grief and the acceptance of sympathy and group support from the family and community.

In rites, rituals, and ceremonies, both secular and specialized, the behavior is highly purposeful. Almost always there seems to be a carefully planned effort to give people a chance to act out feelings too deep to be put into words.

The ceremonial processes also provide a wide range of communication. They start with the assumption that everyone involved understands the meaning of what is going on. Explanations are unnecessary for the language of the ceremony has a universal quality. Usually various art forms are used, and they are a complete language in themselves. Most formal ceremonies use buildings with specialized architecture, music that communicates directly to the emotions, traditional practice that carries the affirmation of a long history, and other contributions of the arts such as dance, costume, and poetry.

In nearly all forms of ceremonial behavior there is a special use of music. For patriotic events there are marching bands with stirring patriotic themes. At weddings there can be organ music, hesitant for the prelude but affirmative and triumphant for the recessional. With a simple service such as the baptism, christening, or dedication of a child, there may be quiet and meditative music appropriate for confronting the mystery of the creation of a new human personality. At funerals there is usually somber and solemn music that invites one to contemplate the meaning of life and death.

Each ceremony also seems to include a specialized type of parade. This parade may be as simple as the walk of the parents from their places in the congregation to the altar for the dedication of their child. Or it may be the bride's march down the aisle to the point where she meets her beloved. For the funeral it is the march from the deathbed to the burial ground. For the patriotic or national event there is the inevitable parade with dignitaries. The parade may have religious overtones as with a Mardi Gras, or be a worship of nature as with the Rose Bowl parade. But whatever the case, there is a deliberate effort to employ the large muscle systems of the participants.

Sociologists call these events rites of passage. They symbolize the movement through life, marking growth, change, and dissolution. Anthropologists examine these events for their usefulness to those who have invested the rites with meaning and gain value from them. Geoffrey Gorer, the English anthropologist, finds that the more elaborate and significant the rites at the time of death, the more quickly people resolve their grief. These ceremonial activities are a response to the deep emotions that accompany crisis events.

Ceremonial acting out meets the needs of the total person— the mind, the emotions, and the body are all involved. The meaning of the event speaks to a person's mental needs and the language of ceremony often carries deep insight that nourishes the mind. At the same time it provides an atmosphere where deep feelings will be at home. Joy and sadness, elation or commitment, are made appropriate by the relationship of the event to the crises of life. The use of various forms of parade makes it possible for people to do something physical, using the large muscle system; this helps to move them beyond sluggishness and depression. It also usually is a symbol of the direction in which life is moving.

Ceremonial acting out is usually public, and the larger the number of people who participate the more valid the emotional release. People support each other in this way by providing a climate appropriate for emotional expression. This affirms the importance of the group to the individual and the individual to the group. The acting out process is a form of group insurance: When you are in trouble or in ecstasy your feelings are important to others, and when they are in trouble or in ecstasy you respond to their need. The movement toward private forms of ceremony may indicate a lack of awareness of the social significance of acting out and of the importance of group support in crises.

Gorer suggests that the more varied the opportunities for ceremonial acting out, the more therapeutic the response. Where people were deeply involved in traditional forms of ritual, the benefits appeared to be extensive. Where there was a wide variety of acting out possibilities—a wealth of formal as well as informal ritualization—the varied needs of various people appeared to be well served.

Alvin Toffler, in his book, *Future Shock,* talks about the losses we suffer as a result of rapid change. An important one is the separation of people from traditional ceremonies. This implies that the therapeutic benefits get lost in the shuffle. It calls for a new resourcefulness, imagination, and inventiveness to put back into life the processes that can serve our valid needs in changing times.

If we develop new forms of ceremonial behavior, we should design them to speak to the whole person and to use as many forms of communication as possible. Their meaning should be so clear that interpretation is unnecessary. The spectator role should be avoided; acting out is more useful when the total person is totally engaged. The acting out should be in the context of a social activity that provides an accepting climate for the emotions and fortifies the group communication with universally understood art forms.

Forms of ceremonial acting out may be the most easily accessible and most useful resource we have for meeting crises. Ritual has deep roots in human racial wisdom. It speaks directly to the whole person about needs that may not be primarily intellectual or rational.

In *Age of Discontinuity* Peter Drucker suggests that men may be overwhelmed by the crises of life if they lose the perceptions that tie life together, present with past and present with future. In basic and archetypal ways the racial wisdom may be preserved and made accessible by the rites, rituals, and ceremonies we have developed.

When we become so rational that we decide what is valid merely by how much sense it makes or how much it costs, we will have reduced life to a mechanized and dehumanized level. Our need for emotional support in times of crisis is often at a nonrational level but it is important none the less.

If people are denied the opportunity to act out their feelings in times of crisis, the alternative may be "acting in," where the organism acts out through physical symptoms what it did not have a chance to do in a healthful, emotional way. An example of this is ulcerative colitis, as discussed in an earlier chapter.

When we appreciate the therapeutic values of acting out our deepest feelings, we are making available to life a resource that is greater than chemical sedation, greater than rational escape, greater than social denial. We are using the full spectrum of human needs and human response within the center of our capacity for communication and relationship. And that is where people grow in understanding and responsiveness.

21

The Therapy of Counseling

People with problems are constantly being advised to go to a counselor and talk it all out. Advice columnists often suggest that a problem cannot be solved via the column and that professional help is needed. I have spent many thousands of hours doing counseling, and I know that important things can be accomplished through the counseling relationship. But, in order to gain the best results from the time and effort spent in counseling, there are conditions that must be met and processes that should be wisely understood.

Counseling is a process. In most instances it involves a trained professional and an individual who is facing a crisis. Many of the benefits of counseling are on occasion gained from relationships that do not involve professionals. People may talk things over with their friends, spouse, or children and feel better afterward. Some of the values of counseling can emerge from such informal processes. However, there are hazards with this informal approach. Personal crises are too important to explore with people who may be ill-informed or just plain gossips.

In order to get the greatest benefits from a counseling relationship, it is important to keep in mind that counseling is not magic and will entail some hard work. The readiness of the person being counseled and his willingness to participate in the process are crucial ingredients in successful counseling.

Often people in crisis have the feeling that the counselor will be able to listen to their sad story, give a few words of golden advice, and make the problem vanish. Quite the opposite is true. The counselor believes in people and their ability to discover resources within themselves; he believes that people can cope with their problems if they are willing to do the hard work of examining them carefully and honestly. With their new insight into themselves and others they will confront the crisis with greater self-assurance and competence.

Professional counselors have prepared themselves to work with people in crises. They seek to do this within a carefully defined framework. Not only do they reject the magical view but they tend to direct the counselee toward mature and responsible action. They respect the privacy of the revelations that develop and use them for the explicit purpose of helping the counselee understand himself and manage himself wisely in relation to his problem. To this end the counselor will expect that the scheduled hours be kept and that the time be used for working diligently at the problem.

It should be clearly understood from the beginning that the success of any counseling relationship rests on the counselee as well as the counselor. The counselee must work to be honest and cooperative. He must work through the inclination to drag his heels and resist the counseling process. He must overcome the inclination to jump to conclusions. It is easy for us to assess blame or pass judgments on other people, but this can be an escape from facing the real problem, and should be avoided. Counselor and counselee should work together in an atmosphere of acceptance and understanding.

It sometimes happens that the process is shifted in midstream. The counselor may decide after he understands more about the counselee that he is not the best person to help and may suggest referral to another. Instead of being considered as failures or defeats these changes may well be considered signs of growth and progress in exposing, exploring, and managing significant personality components.

Essentially, counseling is therapeutic communication. It is important for us to have some insight into how it works. It is also important to understand why at times it does not work as well as we might wish.

Fred made an appointment to talk with a counselor. When he arrived he seemed apprehensive, looked all around him before sitting down, and did not say a word until the door was closed. His muscle activity indicated tension and stress. In a confidential tone he began talking about his problem, a fear of homosexual tendencies. The more he talked, the freer he became. The counselor listened attentively and said very little. When the flow of communication slowed up, the counselor used an open-ended question to start it moving again. For over an hour Fred poured out his fears, his feelings, and his stress. Then Fred thanked the counselor for his help and advice and said he felt much better. Actually the counselor had given no advice. He had said nothing that could even remotely have been considered advice. Why then did Fred think he had received useful guidance and advice?

The dynamic forces at work in counseling are apt to be so powerful for the counselee that it is hard for him to realize how much psychological movement has taken place within himself. Fred had stated his fears. As soon as he had put them into words, however, what he said did not seem quite right. So in effect he said that he wanted to take that back and restate it. During the course of the hour he made statements, heard them, judged them as inadequate, withdrew them, restated them, and was aware of the progress taking place in his thinking. He was so involved in the process of listening to himself and evaluating his utterances that he did not feel separate from the counselor who listened with such interest and concern. One of the more important tasks the counselor performs is that of listening to another with so much investment of self that he becomes a sounding board off which the counselee bounces his words. The counselor learns to accept thanks for what he has done indirectly—as a person receives the compliment of being listened to attentively while he speaks, adjusting his thoughts to his feelings in an experimental fashion.

Sometimes the counselee cannot accept the counseling process. Deep within his being, over a long period of time, he has developed certain defenses. Often they involve self-deception or denial. Cindy was having trouble with her marriage. She sought help from a counselor. As she entered the door, she started describing her husband as a man without feeling, cruel and heartless. She accused, condemned, and criticized him for everything imaginable. After about half an hour of this explosion of negative feeling toward her husband, the counselor asked quietly if she would like to tell him about her father. She started to talk about how wonderful her father was, how handsome he was, and how everyone respected him. Then she went on laughingly to describe some of his business practices and explained how he was able to put things over on stupid people. She believed this ruthless behavior to be quite clever. The counselor quietly asked her to restate what she had said about her father's behavior toward people who were trusting and at his mercy. She jumped up and stamped out of the counseling room, calling the counselor a rather foul name as she left.

Two days later Cindy called to apologize and schedule another appointment. This time she came in in a rather subdued mood, talked quietly and bitterly about her father and how much she had hated him. He had exploited everyone for his own purposes, never loved anyone but himself, and made life so miserable for all of the family that they tried every possible means of escape. When the counselor explored with Cindy her feelings toward other men, she recounted a series of painful affairs where her own distrust had hurt her. When the subject returned to her husband, she again became hostile and explosive and left the counseling room with the assertion that she knew her husband well enough to hate him for what he was. Her defenses of her father had been penetrated so deeply that she felt too vulnerable. She was not ready to have her attitude toward her husband penetrated in a similar way; she was afraid of getting hurt. She did not continue the counseling.

Each person builds into his armament for living a defensive structure that can protect him against the things most apt to injure him. These mechanisms of defense are one of the more difficult problems to manage in a counseling process. They cannot be broken down too rapidly, as they were in the above story, for that leaves the counselee with a vulnerability he cannot tolerate. The counseling process moves slowly, at a speed compatible with the building of more mature and reasonable defenses. When a person has long hidden behind defenses that may include modesty, self-deception, denial, or self-deprecation, it may be difficult or impossible for him to move out from behind the defenses all at once. Resistance in the counseling process should be an indication for the counselor of the need to approach certain areas carefully. One of the tasks of the skilled counselor is to measure carefully the tempo at which the counselee is able to move toward the resolution of his crisis.

People sometimes retreat from the counseling process because it is painful for them. It may be that they hesitate to enter the relationship at all out of a fear of self-exposure, invasion of privacy, or the counselor's judgment. Or, once involved in the process, they may want to run away from what they begin to discover about themselves and others. The movement toward honesty can be threatening because it means confronting a painful reality. A partial step in the counseling process can relieve enough strain so that the person is willing to make another effort at adaptation on his own.

But when the process works therapeutically it is usually because certain significant things take place. Freud's insight into the value of communication showed that words serve to externalize what is going on inside an individual. When a person talks about what is bothering him, there appears to be a release of tension and stress. A skillful listener can give resonance to the communication; this often has the effect of giving it direction. This may support healthful feelings and modify or relieve unhealthy feelings. The release from stress often makes it possible to redirect life energy toward more valid expressions. This in turn further reduces the stress.

The counselee feels better after the counseling process for several reasons. He has moved out of the isolation that usually accompanies inner crisis by sharing it with another. This sharing reduces the anxiety that goes with crisis; he is no longer carrying it all alone. Seeing that the other person is not overwhelmed by the crisis tends to bring it into clearer focus; this also leads toward reduction of anxiety about it. Ventilating the problem relieves pressure much as the lancing of a boil relieves the pain and stress. And the insight that is gained gives new perspective on the problem. Seeing it in a new light may well give it a different look. It may now be possible to approach it with greater capacity for effective management.

The crises that may be helped by counseling come in varied form. Some are primarily quests for information. When a young person is concerned about what college would best serve his educational needs, he seeks out a college counselor whose business it is to know about colleges, their programs, and their requirements. Perhaps the student is concerned about vocational choice. Here again it may be mainly a matter of information, supplemented by the aptitude tests the counselor may give. Such tests can help a counselee understand his own skills and personality traits better, and relate them to his vocational possibilities.

Some counseling is more concerned with insight than with information. Take the case of a student who is troubled by poor study habits, depression, and an inability to relate to the other sex. He seeks help in exploring the area of his personality that causes him distress. Many of the students I counsel are emerging from the intense preoccupation with self that characterizes adolescence. They want reassurance concerning their own emotional growth. A girl may say, "I'm a virgin. Does that mean there is something wrong with me?" Or a boy may say, "Girls turn me off. Does that mean I'm abnormal?" Often talking with a mature and accepting person who is reassuring brings the problem into focus.

Sometimes counseling centers specifically on a crisis. The person has gotten into serious trouble and wants to find a way out. It may be unfinished business of adolescence confronting an adult. Joe came complaining that he was always getting into trouble with people. He described himself as good-natured, fun-loving, and always ready to share a joke. Further exploration showed that his idea of a joke was a childish prank aimed at other people. For instance he would disconnect spark plug wires in the cars of his colleagues at the factory and then couldn't understand why they were angry. He would shove a potato in an exhaust pipe and enjoy the puzzlement of the driver who couldn't get his car started. He once put a bull frog in the desk of the secretary in the front office. It took a lot of work for Joe to be able to understand that he was acting out hostility in a camouflaged manner, and that he did it this way because he was too immature to admit and manage his hostilities in an adult way. With time he learned that practical jokes are really quite impractical and basically childish ways of taking advantage of innocent people. He had to learn to cope with his submerged hostility before he could cope with his real anger toward the people he abused.

Most people use the therapeutic counseling process for education in human growth. We do not arrive at maturity all at once. For instance, we may become physically mature well in advance of emotional maturity. This disparity in the growth process often makes for maladjustment and maladaptive behavior—which needs to be seen for what it is before it can be corrected. Janet, on the other hand, was attractive, older than she looked, and always at work to try to reassure herself that she was youthful and alluring. Her exhibitionistic qualities were immediately observed and noted by a counselor. She had a real problem relating to her neurotic guilt which she could not seem to manage. After several sessions she asked, "Why is it you haven't wanted to talk about sex?" I replied that I would be glad to consider it when it seemed relevant and useful. She said she wanted to talk about sex right then. So I asked her what she wanted to say about it. She actually had nothing to say; she had really been using sex as a ploy to gain attention and superficial satisfaction as a perpetual adolescent. This led into a fruitful examination of her game-playing activities and feelings of guilt about them.

Counseling can also be employed to help give direction to

life. Sometimes we are confused and lose perspective, and the future looks black. This happens frequently after life has suffered a severe blow. Counseling can help us look at ourselves and the course of life to gain a new sense of direction. Counseling after an acute grief experience may be a valued resource in putting the broken pieces of life together. When the future is seen for what it is, it becomes a chance for more living rather than a threat to existence.

Often counseling can be used to gain strength for living. When inner conflict uses up the energy of life for no good purpose it is important to find a resolution and release the misused strength to serve life rather than disrupt it.

During a time when the crises of life arise frequently or unexpectedly, it is important for us to realize that counseling resources are available to us. Guidance counselors, vocational counselors, marriage counselors, pastoral counselors, psychologists, psychiatrists, and other professionals stand ready to aid with the problems of adjustment to uncertainty and stress. It is no sign of great strength to avoid the help we need; rather, it is a sign of strength. Having assessed our needs, we can feel free to move toward help in managing them wisely. The newly refined but old resource of therapeutic communication may ease the pain and hasten the healing of many of life's wounds.

22

The Therapy of Group Action

Increasingly in our day people who confront crises look to group experiences to try to learn coping skills. There are few cities of any size that do not have encounter groups, sensitivity groups, and other groups that offer potentially therapeutic benefits.

How did all this interest in groups come about? There have been a number of contributing factors, and many of them quite accidental. At a mental hospital in Paris years ago two young physicians observed that the patients who were so poor that they could not afford private rooms and had to live in wards made better progress than those in private rooms. They concluded that there was something taking place in the group exchange that was health-restoring.

At a hospital in Massachusetts a number of patients with tuberculosis were brought together to talk about their feelings, their needs, and their resources for helping care for themselves. They made rapid progress toward health. During World War II when psychiatrists were few and so-called "flight fatigue" was common, as an economy measure the patients were brought together to be helped in groups. When it was found that they did much better in groups than they had done in individual therapy, the entire Air Force program for treating emotional disturbances was modified.

In a London hospital that serves people considered beyond medical intervention, a six-bed ward has been incorporated into the hospital. This seems to be the most beneficial ward size for therapeutic purposes, apparently because it approximates the family unit and provides a climate for communication and satisfying relationships.

These and other observations indicating the helpful effects of group processes have stimulated an interest in discovering what it is about the group process that is beneficial. Theoreticians have posited that so many of life's disturbing problems are related to groups that it would be natural for the solutions also to be developed in the group.

If we stop to think about it, we know that life is filled with small group relationships. We begin life in a family and we develop it in classes. We play together in athletic groups, we do role playing in dramatics groups, we work together in offices, we serve on committees—and when all that is over we go home again to the basic form of group life. It does not seem at all strange, then, that we might try to solve problems and develop skills in managing crises together in groups.

Informal types of group therapy have long been used. Years ago our grandmothers gathered together for quilting bees. The men came together for barn raisings. These small groups did useful tasks at the same time they were providing an atmosphere for venting feelings, sharing life experience, and gaining perspective on self and others. If the informal group functioned well, it is reasonable to think that refined and improved methods would serve even better.

What are the major differences between individual counseling and group counseling? In individual counseling the counselor attempts to be accepting and uncritical in order to establish rapport, so that the newly gained progress of the counseling relationship can be sustained and employed in relation to others. In the group, members may be critical of each other yet still not threaten the group process—for this gives everyone a chance to react to others and try out new attitudes as they develop.

In individual counseling the counselee works out his crises with a counselor who is an emotional focus for him, an authority figure like a father or mother. But in the group many personalities are involved. The process of relating to them is more apt to follow the dynamic pattern of sibling rivalry and other elements of the family emotional structure.

In his relationship to a counselee the counselor may adopt a permissive attitude in order to demonstrate his faith in a person who needs to grow in insight and self-confidence. But in the group process this rapport with the leader is less important; in fact, the rejection of the leader by the group may be an important step in group growth.

The dynamics of individual counseling are perhaps more intense and less varied. Resistance and resentment are often sharply defined; it takes a skilled therapist to deal with them effectively. Within the group, emotional responses are apt to be more varied and less intensely *focused* because the feelings can be spread over a larger number of persons. In a group the feeling is focused less on the therapist, and is therefore diffused, though not reduced.

The benefits of the group process are often more immediately accessible for the counselee for he must start to react with the group at once. With individual counseling he may postpone acting on his new insights by intellectualizing about them. So change in a group setting is likely to be more rapid and also more apt to confirm itself in action.

The group process allows for a more rapid and complete exposure to the feelings of others. In the last decade or two new and more dramatic forms of group procedure have begun to be explored. These new techniques have moved beyond a concern for verbalization and so-called head trips and are largely preoccupied with person-to-person emotional experience.

These new experiments have attempted to cut through sham and hypocrisy with the goal of developing the individual's capacity for love, trust, and emotional growth. Sometimes these groups take place at a retreat center remote from urban turmoil. Participants are encouraged to have a sustained experience of knowing one another in depth. The particular practices that are employed vary depending on the leader and makeup of the group. Some groups are religiously oriented and work to put into practice the neglected precepts of creed. Others are concerned with breaking through defenses; they may use techniques of body massage, touching, and nude encounter in swimming pools.

A brief look at some of the techniques employed might make it easier to decide which would best serve your personal needs and inclinations.

Some more traditional groups use simple methods of self-examination within an atmosphere of mutual acceptance and common interest. Alcoholics Anonymous has been doing this for some time. The group's common problem immediately establishes a bond among the members. In the *closed group* all is secret and confidential. In the *open group* there is an effort to reach others who may have the problem but are not yet ready to cope with it honestly. The Alanon groups are made up of spouses of alcoholics; they are designed to give insight into the problem as well as support in meeting it. Synanon has a similar program designed to meet the needs of those with a drug problem.

Parents without Partners tries to meet the needs of the widow or widower with children, the separated or divorced person, and the unmarried mother. These are short-term sessions whose purpose is to share common problems and seek resources for managing them. A similar program is followed by THEO (They Help Each Other) for the grief-stricken. The Widow to Widow program is an even more specific group.

Some continuing groups are conducted by psychotherapists who use role-playing, psychodrama, and films and lectures to gain insight and information as well as skills in coping with the various problems of group membership. Group discussion and participation are basic to group activity.

Some group methods are built around special techniques, as are "primal groups." Based on Arthur Janov's theory, they work to stimulate the "primal scream." The effect of the scream is to release emotional blocks that have been impeding personality development. Encounter groups use a similar method of having people act out their aggression by pillow pounding and other substitute acts. These methods frequently result in rapid psychological movement. However, they are not without hazard. When the defenses are stripped away too rapidly, the person is highly vulnerable. When he leaves the accepting group and goes back into an environment that is not aware of his needs, he may suffer psychic injury.

Sensitivity groups are to a great extent exploratory. They usually combine their explorations with a strong measure of supportiveness. Their methods may be more gradual, although there is no set pattern and no two groups function along exactly the same lines. The group's makeup and the leader's attitudes tend to set the guidelines.

Marathon groups of all kinds make use of the effects of time and fatigue on interactions between people. Usually they meet for a period of constant encounter for a weekend, and the members of the group work together until their fatigue and the lowering of their resistance to each other causes emotional breakthroughs that are often highly significant. Even the minimarathons that last from six to eight hours allow more time to work through thoughts and feelings than is the case with most encounter group sessions, which last for two or three hours. The marathons usually do not stop for formal meals but have a buffet available for sandwiches and coffee at all times. Informality prevails. Members lie on the floor or take any other position that suits them. The important thing is to pay attention to each other and keep the process of reacting at work. Sometimes in the early hours of the morning a person will perceive himself and others in a new light, and the insight will serve to open new doors of consciousness.

The important point in any group encounter is to experience "being in the world" in larger measure. This means being in relation to the other people in your world in a more vigorous way. It means becoming more alive in yourself and in your encounters with others.

In any group activity the important matter to consider is what happens to the participants. Over the years I have seen many significant forms of growth take place in a variety of small group activities. I have watched businessmen see their colleagues as people for the first time and become concerned about their feelings, their families, their aspirations, and their human dimensions. I have seen widows who felt lost and lonely discover a new life in the shared experiences of other widows. I have seen divorced people move beyond their feelings of guilt and failure to find a new and more mature love. I have seen people humiliated by alcoholism find the strength to become new and creative persons. I have seen people addicted to hard drugs go "cold turkey" and find the strength to move through their turmoil to personal victory. I know there is power in the impact of a group stimulus.

How does the stimulus for new growth manifest itself? Glenn, a lawyer, came into an encounter group filled with doubts about such activity. He was depressed because of the recent death of his wife of many years. He was urged to attend a group session with the admonition that it would certainly do him no harm. The group happened to be made up of professionals in psychotherapy. After some time in disciplined thinking and meditation he was asked to take a chair in the middle of a circle. He was invited to relax and let the other group members hold him in loving concern in order to welcome him back in fuller life. For fifteen minutes a dozen psychologists and therapists who had spent years training themselves in disciplined meditation centered their loving thoughts on Glenn. When the quarter-hour was over, Glenn looked around him in disbelief. With a radiant smile on his face he said that he had never been so filled with feelings of warmth and love. He has moved out of his grief and despair and has not missed a session of the group since his first unwilling step to join it. What happened to Glenn? We can conjecture many things. We can say he found much needed emotional support. We can say he discovered new friends. We can say he broke through the shell of his depression. We can say he was at just the right moment to end his mourning and discover that he was still alive. But whatever we say in explanation, we cannot completely encompass the new feelings that Glenn discovered that day and has not lost since.

Fred was a research physicist at a national research center. He was attending a conference of people interested in exploring the nature of consciousness. When he came to the conference, he could not even carry his own traveling bags. For years he had had a back condition so serious that it practically immobilized him. He was able to lift nothing and stepped about with great care lest he jar his spine. Although a young man, he acted like a decrepit old man. During the conference he asked a group of people who were highly disciplined in the use of their psychic energy to lay their hands on him. As he sat in a chair, Fred's friends gathered around him on all sides. Some sat on the floor and held his feet and legs. Others stood behind and beside him, placing their hands on his head, shoulders, and arms. They remained in silence together for fifteen or twenty minutes. When they concluded their session together, Fred stretched to his full height and moved as he had not been able to for several years. Two days later he was throwing bags to the top of the bus and handling heavy suitcases without pain.

As a researcher Fred was not able to explain what had happened. Others suggested that he had been able to break through an emotional stress that had produced spasticity in the spinal muscles. Others said he seemed to have responded to some accumulation of psychic energy that was let loose in his body. Still others claimed that there must have been a psychogenic cause for his ailment which was removed by a stronger psychic impulse at work. Fred's behavior, however, seemed more significant than any of the theories employed to explain it. Fred merely commented that there seemed to be something at work.

Glenn and Fred are both professionals, well trained in rational thought and careful observation. Something happened to them in a group that changed them in significant ways. Small groups in action have been doing things like this down through history, and increasingly in our day small groups can modify the lives of their members. Racially mixed groups discover meanings in each other's lives that move them beyond crippling prejudice. Church groups find spiritual resources that had long lain dormant. Business groups find new meanings for their individual and collective lives. The small group has power to change life in many ways.

When the crises of life weigh you down, it is important to know that there are resources available to give support, spiritual strength, and impulses toward true wholeness of being. We may not understand all about how groups work, but there is no denying their power. It may be that the reservoirs of meaning in our humanness are never fully discovered until we become a part of a group process that emphasizes our humanity. And in an increasingly dehumanizing society it can be a most important influence for us.

23

Anticipating Crises

Is there some way people can prepare for crises so that they will not do so much damage? Is there some skill that can be developed in advance to ease people through these times of turbulence?

Sociologist Dr. Robert Fulton thinks we can give positive answers to questions like these. He has found that it is possible to take a defensive stance against the most devastating form of crisis if one has the wisdom and courage to do so.

Fulton explored the nature of anticipatory grief, and found that when certain people are able to look ahead at an event, no matter how distressing it may be, they go through a process of preparation that helps them meet the event with greater strength. But he finds that this is the case only with people who are willing to be honest with themselves about the crisis. If, instead of facing the crisis, a person tries to look the other way, to deny its existence and ignore its impact on his life, he is likely to make himself even more vulnerable.

Anticipatory grief, like the management of any other form of acute deprivation, calls for facing reality and withdrawing the emotional investment with as little self-injury as possible. This should be done with skill and insight; if done in a state of emotional panic, it may prematurely fracture relationships.

Jessica was the wife of an Air Force pilot assigned to duty in Southeast Asia. She was so filled with anxiety that she dreamed night after night of plane crashes and fiery explosions. She suffered so much anticipatory grief that without really knowing what was happening she withdrew her emotional investment in her husband. She went through a period of mild euphoria where she felt release from worry and a deep sense of inner peace. At first she thought she had found a faith to sustain her. But when her husband finally returned home and she found she had no feeling for him, she began to realize that something had taken place within her. She had resolved her grief by a devastating emotional separation. Jessica had gone through a mourning process in anticipation of the fact, and the fact did not materialize. With counseling Jessica was led to understand what had happened. She was obliged to go through another period of courting, falling in love again and reinvesting her emotions where they had been before she went through the withdrawal process.

At a hospital where a number of children with leukemia were treated, an emotional drama involving anticipatory grief was studied. Complaints from the nurses led to the study. The nurses said the parents seemed to turn against their own children, abandoning them to the love and care of the nursing staff. Let us take one mother as an example.

Sophia was deeply disturbed when her eight-year-old son became ill. She took him to the family physician who gave a thorough physical with careful blood studies. He called Sophia and her husband in for a conference and said that it seemed quite certain that their son had leukemia. Sophia was distraught. She sought out another physician and got a confirming diagnosis. She sought out specialists nearby and far away. She went through a frantic process of trying to deny the painful news. Finally her son had to be hospitalized. She was at his bedside for many hours each day watching the course of his symptoms with complete attention. One day a member of the hospital staff asked if she would be willing to help raise funds for a leukemia research foundation. She immediately agreed and soon was pouring her energy, skill, and attention into a task that seemed to help her face the threat of leukemia in general rather than specific terms.

As her son's condition grew progressively worse, Sophia gave more of herself to the foundation work. The nurses complained among themselves that Sophia did not come in as often and stayed but a short while. In fact they thought that she was abandoning her son when he needed her the most. When he died, she showed no emotion and shed no tears. In contrast members of the nursing staff were deeply involved emotionally, cried freely, and showed strong resentment against Sophia for what they assumed was a hardened attitude toward her child. But it appears that what happened was not so much an abandonment as a working through of anticipatory grief so thoroughly that the emotional capital had been withdrawn from the child and reinvested in work for the foundation. Sophia moved in her own way from concentrating on death to what she felt was a concentration on life.

It is quite obvious from the experiences of Jessica and Sophia that it is possible for anticipatory grief work to go too far too fast and produce inappropriate responses. But having said that, we need to look carefully at the therapeutic benefits that can come from a wise facing of the future and a careful preparation for the crisis events that are sure to be a part of it.

Much philosophy has been based on a desire to give strength to life as we meet the future by creating attitudes in the present. The ancient Stoics made a virtue of controlling emotions so completely that nothing that happened could penetrate their protective shield. So they prepared to endure pain, suffer tragic loss, and face death without showing fear or trying to escape. Essentially the feeling was that to live is to suffer; controlling suffering thus was living with strength and courage. Many people try to build a little stoicism into their lives and often it shows up as a type of fatalism: There are some things you cannot do anything about, so you may as well learn to accept them. What often happens is that this fatalistic thinking so pervades people's lives that they begin to accept without question things they could do something about.

On the other hand there is the often misunderstood philosophy of the Epicureans. They were not so carefree and self-indulgent as often pictured. But they did feel that life was meant to be lived with satisfaction and they tried to learn the skills that would make it possible to avoid suffering and to find fulfillment and satisfaction. Our modern version of this philosophy shows itself in a preoccupation with satisfying appetites, enjoying the present without too much regret for the past or too much concern for the future. In our contemporary form of this old philosophy there is apt to be a type of irresponsibility that is so concerned with the present that little responsible thought is given to the future. In fact, irresponsibility in the present tends to create crises for the future.

Somewhere between the extremes of these two philosophies there can be a middle ground of wise preparation for the problems of the future—not undue anxiety but realistic anticipation. The impulse to "know thyself" and control your behavior can be incorporated into a balanced philosophy. People can be trained to build inner resources for coping with future crises.

One day I had the privilege of interviewing a Sioux brave, Guy-ah-wagawha, who was a fine specimen of manhood as well as quite a mature philosopher. He had been well educated in the white man's schools. This education had led him to appreciate elements of his own heritage and he was a vigorous exponent of Sioux wisdom. As we talked about what made a brave be brave, he told of training methods used in his tribe in early childhood. Some seemed harsh and cruel. He said that when he was six years old his father took him out on a lake on a cold winter's day and, when they were well out, took a firm hold on his hair and lowered him into the freezing water. Having learned not to whimper or scream, he took his dunking quietly and with courage. His father then explained to Guy-ah-waga-wha that he need never again worry about falling into freezing water because he knew what it was like and now he knew he could survive it. The essence of this form of education was preparation for crisis in a matter-of-fact atmosphere that stimulated self-confidence.

If there is anything in our educational process that prepares us for crises, it seems to be a desire to avoid confronting them or anticipating them. At a lecture I gave to a parent-teacher organization about the need for preparing children for meeting crises, one irate mother rose to her feet and announced with conviction, "I'm going to do all I can, as long as I can, to protect my children from facing the painful and cruel aspects of life. I don't care what you or anyone else says—they will have plenty of time for trouble later. Now life should be a time of pleasure." While in one respect we might applaud this woman's sentiments, we could hardly feel she was taking a realistic approach. She was advocating an unrealistic attitude toward life that would ill prepare a child for coping with what was bound to come along in time.

Avery Weisman of Harvard has written extensively on life crises and their management. He speaks of primal anxiety and the need to cope with it. This primal anxiety is part of the inner tension between existence and extinction. The need to avoid the threat of extinction may be so great that it leads to a denial of existence itself. The fear of death may be so great that it pervades all of life and so cripples life. To overcome this form of paralysis, Weisman recommends a type of maturity that is not afraid to look at both sides of the many forms of life polarity. He sees in life not only a pleasure principle but also an unpleasure principle. The effort to control suffering may be more critical than the desire to find pleasure. So a person must come to terms with the potential hazards of life in order to have the wisdom to confront all of life. A philosophy of life that is too small to cope with all of life is inadequate indeed.

In our efforts to deal with the existential hazards of life we may move in quite contradictory directions. Two of the more popular forms of response to crisis may be expansions of personality traits rather than distinct philosophies. Leibnitz long ago said that men are apt to be right in their affirmations and wrong in their negations. Underlying this precept is the idea that when men make affirmations they are apt to be speaking out of their own experience but when they make denials they are trying to defend themselves against the unacceptable aspects of someone else's experience.

Some approaches to crisis management use a mixture of denial and acceptance. This is true of Christian Science and Alcoholics Anonymous, where the ill person denies the reality of his illness by affirming something else that has a greater reality for him. He affirms the unreality of matter so that the afflictions of matter become illusory. In a group the alcoholic affirms the power of group life to support him while he denies the power of his compulsion. In so doing he finds the strength to control his compulsion. Quite simply, this approach accentuates the positive and eliminates the negative. This form of mental and emotional process seems to serve best the personality needs of the person who seeks a new kind of behavior to substitute for the destructive compulsion that produced his crises.

In the analytic approach there is a persistent effort to confront reality and develop the skills needed to work through the problems that are causing the crises. The method employed is similar to that used in certain forms of group therapy where honest confrontation with self and others is stimulated. Questions are asked and answers are sought. Instead of denial and retreat into illusory thinking, the emphasis is on ruthless confrontation.

In all the various methods, the unique needs of the individual are central. A method that works well for one person may not work for another. Each individual tries to discover what will help him develop the strength to handle his problems.

To get started we need to ask ourselves some questions. What hurts most in a crisis? Is it the fracturing of the self or the element of surprise that catches us off balance? Is it the feeling of our inadequacy or is it a feeling of anger and frustration that so little can be done? Is it a feeling of isolation from life and deep loneliness? Is it a great need to reach out for others to whom we may cling in desperation? The answers we give to questions like these will determine the direction we should move in seeking resources that will be especially valid for us.

Each person can build within himself a kind of psychic gyroscope that enables him to manage turbulence without being thrown off course or inundated. If you know sailing vessels, you know the value of lead in the keel. The weight carried on the keel deep underwater determines the height of the mast and the amount of sail that can be carried without danger of capsizing. Preparation for crises is like building a balance deep within that enables us to ride out storms and keep moving ahead. In fact, with enough lead in the keel you can turn a strong wind into forward progress.

In developing the inner skill to cope with future crises, you might try imagining the worst that could happen. If you can manage the worst, then you are set for the lesser events that may happen along the way.

At a Catholic seminary one day I noticed a monk walking back and forth in the cloister with a book in his hand. I looked for quite a while at this person in complete concentration. Finally I made bold to break in on his meditation and ask what he was doing. He said he was contemplating his death. I asked why. He responded that it was a rule of his order that each monk spend some time each day contemplating his own death so that he would be able to value life and live it wisely.

Confronting all the realities of life as far as possible can help to build lead into one's emotional keel. The elements of emotional maturity are easily discerned if we look for them. Many psychologists and psychiatrists have listed their own concepts of what it takes to produce maturity. Here is the essence of some of them:

1. The ability to be guided by reality rather than by fear.
2. Long-term values.
3. A grown-up conscience.
4. Independence.
5. The capacity to give and receive love.
6. A reasonable dependence.
7. A reasonable aggressiveness.
8. Healthy defense mechanisms.

9. Good sexual adjustment with acceptance of one's own gender.

10. Good work adjustment.

Emotional maturity needs to be balanced with intellectual adequacy. A person can learn perspective on life and its problems by cultivating an intelligent curiosity about himself and others even in the presence of turbulent conditions. He can learn to understand why he reacts as he does and to be considerate of his own feelings.

A form of spiritual perspective helps to fit the incidents of life into something larger than the moment. Avery Weisman writes, "If a person facing nothing but death can retain a sense of awe for the inner affinity of existence, and for his own significance, the inevitability of extinction can become a necessary harmonic among the antitheses of life, not just a tragic and meaningless interruption. Much of this task of affirmation and confirmation belongs to the psychiatrist, the physician and those who stand to lose most by the person's death. In mundane, human terms, *agape is acceptance of another person in existential terms.* If this state can be achieved, primary anxiety can yield to reality and responsibility, since nothing is without significance and no act is without motivation."

Historically the great religions have tried to give this spiritual perspective to life. Sometimes it has been in graphic imagery, sometimes in the form of a broad view that makes place for all possibilities. The frame of reference has always been large enough to guarantee that the person happened to the crisis rather than the crisis happening to the person. This is a bold affirmation that no matter what happens in the course of life, the value of the person remains paramount; therefore, the things that happen to him are incidental.

How do we learn to become adequate in anticipating the crises of life? We can practice. We can move toward crises with courage rather than run away from them with fear. Then we will learn the slow but significant skills for managing them.

We can develop skills in contemplation. We can look ahead and experimentally manage events. We are encouraged to drive defensively so that we can be prepared for emergencies on the highway. Why not also learn to live defensively so that we are prepared for the emergencies on the highway of life?

We can look within ourselves and face our desires to run away from life. We can challenge our inner being to grow up to where encounter will take the place of escape and adequacy will replace apprehension.

24

Managing the Aftermath

Crises are hard enough to manage but if we are unprepared to cope with them wisely the aftermath of our crises may be even more difficult. The reason for this is that often, in a period of adjustment, we do not realize what is taking place and so we may make unreasonable demands upon ourselves.

A person may handle himself with great skill in an automobile accident. He may do all the right things in just the right way. When it seems that the whole thing is over, the police have gone, the ambulance has gone, and the wrecker has towed away the damaged car, he falls apart. His nerves give out and he begins to tremble and shake. Why now? If he was able to manage the crisis, why did the aftermath catch him off guard?

We need to remember that the aftermath is part of the crisis. It is a period of readjustment, of bringing the special equipment for meeting crises back into the range of normal living. The anatomical, physiological, anthropological, social, and psychological resources that have been marshaled to cope with the crisis now have to settle back into their normal forms of functioning. This cannot happen all at once, and it cannot happen without involving the entire person.

The crew of a combat plane might function with perfect discipline and competence in battle, but once safely back on the ground the strain breaks through. Men go through long periods of confinement in prison camps, maintaining high morale and goodwill toward each other, only to give way to conflict, charges, and countercharges as soon as they have been released. What is happening?

Everything that happens to us is registered in the depths of our being and becomes a part of us. When we go through a period of stress and emerge from it, it has had its impact on us. In subtle and unobserved ways, we have become a different person.

We have seen people go through major surgery and meet the crisis of pain, physical adaptation, and adjustment admirably. But during the long and restricted period of recuperation they became irritable and restless, complaining constantly. What was going on?

The physical organism has its own built-in defensive mechanisms that guard us from actions that might be injurious to full recovery. George, a gymnast, fell and broke his arm. It was a clean break with no complications and after a few weeks his arm was as good as new. He wanted to get back to work and his physician gave him permission. But something inside of him was reluctant to let him go back to work. In the past he had concentrated so completely on what he was doing that he was free from fear. But now he found himself so afraid that he was ashamed. He tried to control his fear by making himself do what he did not want to do, but found that this only increased his inner conflict and further immobilized him. So George returned to his physician to get help. The physician explained that the system's built-in defenses work psychologically and at their own time schedule. While the bone may have knitted perfectly and quickly, the psychological defenses were apparently going at a different pace. George was urged to go slowly, place limited demands on his muscle system, and gradually work back to the level of performance he had reached before the fall. This he did and six months later he was performing better than ever. When he was asked the exact time when the change came about, he could not place it for it was gradual and imperceptible. To be kind to ourselves, we need to know this other process and adjust to it.

Often it seems that illness changes personality. A person who has been demanding and authoritarian may become submissive. A person who has been good-natured may become hostile and grouchy. A past method for meeting life situations may be modified for the crisis becomes a major life situation and the old ways of coping may not function as expected or as effectively.

Much the same process is at work with acute grief. A person may find inner strength to face the tragic events that occur, but, a few weeks later, be unable to function. Franklin was a funeral director. He observed people in grief day after day, and confronted the most difficult events in the life of the community with poise and professional competence. Franklin's grandson was a bright lad with great promise. It was decided to send him to a college in a northern city because a black student might have greater opportunity to develop there. There, one evening after studying for a while, Franklin's grandson decided to walk downtown for a hamburger and a cup of coffee. A group of young ruffians from a nearby town had been cruising about in their car looking for a defenseless black. They assaulted him and beat him to death.

Some time later, Franklin told me of his reactions. First, he made all the funeral arrangements for the service that he felt fitting for his martyred grandson. He said he did everything with composure and professional competence. But the day after the funeral he had an overwhelming reaction against his own funeral home. He said he didn't care what happened to anyone else in trouble. He just folded up for six months and never once went near his establishment. Then, at the end of this long period, he felt different inside, and returned to carry on his professional activities as before. But for the six-month period something in the core of his being was out of control. He had to listen to this other force, which apparently was protecting his lacerated emotional state from more stress than it could tolerate. Only when the period of adjustment had been completed was he set free to go about the tasks of life.

Erich Lindemann has pointed out that the most difficult period in adjusting to acute grief often comes ten days to two weeks after the tragic event. This is the point where social support and the presence of other people are usually withdrawn, as they must return to their own homes and tasks. The bereaved person then has to face alone the hundred and one small losses that manifest themselves when the fabric of life is torn apart. Often the full impact of loss is felt when you start to say something to someone who is not there, when you long for a companionship that has been taken for granted for so long, when you come to decide on a lonely vacation or go to a concert alone. And these are the times when adjustment takes place. Coping with the full dimensions of this withdrawal of emotional investment takes some wisdom.

Often under the stress of emotion we do things that may not be wise as far as the aftermath is concerned. Elana felt she was a sophisticated person who did not need the benefit of what she felt were sentimentalities and emotional ceremonials. When her husband died suddenly, she called a funeral director and told him she wanted no service, no notice in the paper, and not even a moment of formal ceremonial farewell. She explained that her husband was dead and there was nothing that could be done to bring him back; the funeral director should get rid of the useless body in any way he felt was appropriate and she would go on with living. Within six months Elana sought a counselor. She said she could not go through another day without help. Every time the telephone rang or the mailman came, she wanted to scream. She felt she could not answer the doorbell. Each day it seemed that one of her friends or her husband's friends heard of the sad event and wanted to express sympathy, almost always with some remark that was indirectly accusing. They would say, "I don't know why it was I didn't hear earlier, but I just did." Thinking she would spare herself some grief, in effect Elana separated herself from the help she needed. In facing this painful emotional event, she could have had emotional support from her friends, and an opportunity to confront them openly and honestly as they all experienced together the feelings that were appropriate. Now months later she realized that she had been unkind to herself but could not go back and do things over in a wiser way. She had to go through a counseling process that helped her encounter her nonrational behavior, understand it, and move beyond its impact on her life.

The aftermath of illness, accident, and death is matched by the emotional repercussions that accompany post-partum emotional states, separation, divorce, parental feelings of abandonment by children, and forms of life-modifying disability (physical, psychological, and social). Here we have the basic conditions of an identity crisis. We need to understand the nature of withdrawal symptoms and the valid forms of treatment.

When a baby is born prematurely, its physical system is obliged to adjust to external circumstances for which it is not ready. This calls for all kinds of special help at the physical level —but special help is also needed in the personality development, at a later age, to manage the out-of-context events of life.

Being jilted in love is painful. There has been a steady build-up of self-commitment and expectation, idealized hopes, and perhaps extravagant dreams. Then when it all comes tumbling down at once the system may be so deeply injured that it never recovers. We all know people who suffered an unhappy love affair and were never again able to run the risks involved in making a commitment to love. The aftermath of an identity crisis may be so difficult that it permanently scars life.

Henry had been employed by his company for twenty-eight years. When it was bought out by a large industrial combine, he felt secure in his position. He had worked his way up and had a good pension in prospect. Then the new conglomerate sent in its efficiency experts to assess the newly acquired company. They discovered that they could save lots of pension money in the future if they terminated the employment of personnel before their thirtieth year of service. So, because of a surplus of executive personnel, major changes had to be made.

Henry and a number of other minor executives were to be provided with the benefits of early retirement. They were honored at a special dinner meeting, given fine wristwatches, and thanked for their loyal service to the company. Henry understood the meaning of this move, and was embittered by it. He moved to Florida where he thought he could live more reasonably on his sharply curtailed pension and got a part-time job in a delicatessen making sandwiches during the noon rush hours. The man who had been secure and trusting has become bitter, cynical, and almost constantly depressed. Nothing really matters for him and he is moving toward a life of meaninglessness and possibly a premature death. The aftermath of the unwelcomed retirement has caused an emotional letdown comparable to his economic letdown.

It would be the unusual life that was marked by constant success and good fortune. Every life must build some skills in coping with failure. Unfortunate things are bound to happen, but they need not terminate the forward movement of life.

How can a person learn to fail gracefully? One of the benefits of sports and games is that they make it possible to try hard, lose a game, and still congratulate the winner. With games there is always another day to play. With life there is also the future —if the doors are not slammed in its face.

In facing failure it is always wise to be kind to yourself. You are the only self you have. So often people become their own worst enemies because they cannot tolerate their inability to function as they would like. Even when they might be tolerant of others and treat them kindly in times of misfortune and disappointment, they do not seem able to do the same for themselves. When difficulties arise, it is basic to give yourself the breaks you would expect for others. It is essential to stand off and look at yourself objectively. Understand what is going on inside you so you can accept yourself and your behavior under stress. You would not expect a man to run with a broken leg. It is no more reasonable to expect a person to function normally with a broken heart.

Sometimes it is difficult to understand ourselves because we are so close to our own feelings; we may tend to see them through a distorted perspective. Actions may so camouflage emotions that we do not easily comprehend the meaning of our own behavior. After an unfortunate marriage and divorce, Warren felt lonely and at loose ends. He almost immediately sought the company of another person and without too much opportunity for true acquaintance he married again. Almost before the honeymoon was over he discovered that his new wife had many of the same objectionable traits as his first wife. Why had he been so blinded by his emotions? The fracturing of a love relationship, however valid it may seem, releases ambivalent responses. While intellectually he was willing to admit the need for separation from his first wife, emotionally he still sought her out—or at least elements of her personality. Instead of resolving an emotional problem, his obscure feelings compounded it.

Often the aftermath of a crisis is delayed for so long that it is not recognized for what it really is. This is often the case with children. The emotional crisis of early childhood may be restored at other phases of the growth process in ways that do not at first appear to be related. For example, Jane, now fifteen, feels great hostility and resentment toward her father, focused on his physical disability. Yet he had developed the crippling illness years before, when she was three years old. What she could not cope with in childhood she is trying to cope with in another and yet inadequate way as an adolescent.

When a person is experiencing the emotional impact of the aftermath of a crisis, it is important to assess it for what it really is. Great failures who have become great successes usually gave themselves plenty of time to explore the meaning of what had happened to them. After a great moment of illumination that was to change the course of his life, St. Paul went into seclusion for two years or more to try to understand what had happened to him and act wisely on it. He had the emotional equivalent of a psychiatrist in the friendship of Barnabas, who spent time exploring with him the crisis and its meaning for his future action.

Henry David Thoreau failed as a school teacher not because

of the students but because of their parents. He was driven back upon himself to explore the meaning of life and society. He built a cabin and lived on Walden Pond for more than three years while he did this work of exploration. He wrote to bring his thoughts and feelings under control, and in so doing he turned the failure into success. The deep introspection of his writing and the honesty of his inner search produced one of the most authentic pieces of American literature. Even now thousands of young people who are trying to understand the flaws in our culture look back at this work of Thoreau, for they find that it helps them see through the hypocrisy in their own day.

The aftermath to a crisis can be an important time for adaptation and change. A crisis of major proportion ends one era of our personal history and points the way toward a new one. If we feel a sense of unwise urgency, we may act without careful consideration and create more problems for ourselves. However, if we take time not only to see what is going on around us but also to explore within ourselves, we will make a better and more creative adjustment.

A crisis can shake our self-confidence. We may pass harsh judgments on ourselves, or even punish ourselves. This is not being true to ourselves. It is not even being fair to ourselves. If there is ever a time when fairness is important, it is when we are trying to restore balance to life, to restore inner equilibrium. The self-criticism that is so often part of the aftermath depressive state should be accepted; it is part of the quest for a new adequacy. This is no time to sell yourself short. Rather it is a time to give yourself the benefit of the doubt, to get perspective on yourself. Then you can move beyond inadequate judgments and look forward to the future with new strength.

25

Crises and Personal Growth

In the preceding chapters we have tried to gain insight into the nature and management of crises. We have looked at the positive and negative impact of crises on the lives of many people. Our ability to cope with crises will be enhanced by knowing as much as we can about them, but knowledge alone is not enough. There is something more than knowledge at work in the depths of our being that aids us in meeting our problems.

We have explored some useful techniques for managing crises, but techniques are not enough. If they are to serve us well, techniques must be built on something else.

What is this other ingredient so essential to managing our crises? We might call it a cosmic perspective.

In the ancient drama of Job, man confronts a variety of overwhelming crises that test his spirit. He suffers illness, deprivation, acute grief, and economic collapse. It seems as if all of creation has turned against him—perhaps it would have been better if he had never been born. Friends say that he has brought his suffering and misfortunes upon himself, but Job knows he has done right and rejects this. One friend suggests that perhaps things are really not so bad—if Job would only think positively it would all go away. Job rejects this, accusing his friend of being superficial and ignorant of the depth of human suffering. Another friend says that tragedy is a part of life and there is nothing a man can do but take it. A youthful friend says he is ashamed of his elders for they fail to see that there may be some cosmic purpose and meaning in man's suffering. And finally a voice from deep in the universe speaks up. The voice of God challenges man and his small perspective; it says that man suffers because he has such a poor concept of the universe. In his ignorance and short-sightedness, man judges the rest of creation from his own limited perspective. The cosmic voice says that man likes what he can use and what serves him well: He approves of horses and cows and sheep for they are useful to him, but does not like crocodiles, hippopotami, and serpents—for he does not understand their place in creation. If man could acquire a cosmic perspective he would see many of the things that trouble him in a different light. He would be able to accept and adjust in a way that would reduce his suffering. A broad and deep perspective on life helps us to interpret whatever happens to us.

There is wisdom in this ancient Jewish tale. When people suffer crises, they frequently take a self-centered, selfish approach to what has happened: They take it personally. The more selfish they become in their sorrow, the more their distress is amplified. When they bring their own experience of suffering into cosmic perspective, it changes.

The person who curses an earthquake is the one who takes it so personally that he does not see beyond it. Looked at from a broader perspective, it is quite clear that life upon the earth is dependent on earthquakes. They are a part of the process that raises up mountains, and creates arable valleys and broad plains. The person who builds his home over an earthquake fault may act in ignorance, but he does himself an injury if he personalizes the earthquake as his enemy. Cosmic patterns are at work for larger goals than an individual's comfort and security.

When Abraham Maslow speaks of a third force operative in human experience, he apparently has in mind the kind of cosmic perspective that can make it possible for a person to feel at home in the universe. When this feeling or philosophical focus is achieved, the universe is seen more as a friend than as an enemy. Then events are not personalized as punishment or individualized assault. Rather they are seen as part of a larger process to which one adapts with acceptance and understanding. When this is done, we can live above the self-centered and personal interpretations that make a person vulnerable to injury.

Where man confronts life and its crises with a concern for greater perspective, he is in a position to experience transcendent meaning. Transcendence may sound like a mysterious process, but actually it is an achievement of understanding that can have intellectual, emotional, or spiritual dimensions.

At the intellectual level transcendence grows with greater knowledge. If, for instance, a bushman in the heart of the Australian wilderness picks up a fuse plug dropped by a prospector, he has no way of identifying it for what it is. He fits it into his experience—to him it may be only an oddly shaped and attractive stone that he will wear as a decoration. Give the same fuse plug to a housewife and she will probably recognize it from past experience. So her knowledge transcends that of the bushman in proportion to her understanding of the nature and use of the object. If, however, we were to show the same item to the production engineer at the manufacturing plant where the fuse plug was made, we would get a vastly different response. This person would know at once the materials employed, the fusing strength of the particular item, the problems of production, and the variety of uses to which it could be put. The engineer's knowledge of the fuse plug would transcend the housewife's because of more extensive experience with it.

The experience of transcendence is always personal because it is bound up with our own knowledge and insight.

But transcendence may also have an emotional dimension. The self-centered person has a capacity for love but it is limited. When a person learns to love others as he loves himself, he develops a measure of emotional transcendence. But when he learns to love life and the cosmic process as he loves himself and others, life gains a transcendent perspective at the emotional level. With this form of perspective a person is not as apt to be injured by the things that happen to him, for he sees them not from a merely selfish point of view but from a cosmic perspective.

What is true of intellectual and emotional transcendence is also true spiritually. When we assume that we are more than the sum of our parts and greater than the total of our experience, then we begin to take a transcendent view of our lives. We look beyond the accumulation of little things that might distress us. We seek a meaning and purpose that is larger than our self-centered philosophical stance. This cosmic dimension sets us free from many of the minor pains of life. We are at home with a larger meaning and a larger purpose that we can see at work everywhere. The philosophy of life that is based on this approach is called cosmic humanism.

Over forty years ago Albert Einstein wrote a little book called *Cosmic Religion.* In it he looks at the sources of inspiration that motivate the scientist's search for transcendent knowledge. He wrote, "Everything that men do or think concerns the satisfaction of the needs they feel or the escape from pain. This must be kept in mind when we seek to understand spiritual and intellectual movements and the way in which they develop. . . . A contemporary has rightly said that the only deeply religious people of our largely materialistic age are the earnest men of research."

Our study of the nature and management of the crises that bring pain into life seeks ways to make the incidental really incidental rather than cataclysmic. This may best be done by seeking a transcendental experience of life. This experience develops to the point where the individual builds an adequate philosophy of life.

A true philosophy of life emerges at the meeting place of a person's cosmology (or concept of the universe) and his psychology (his concept of the nature of man). If he has an inadequate cosmology or psychology, this basic philosophy will not serve him well in crises. Some people think of a cosmic structure presided over by a Being who manipulates the universe so that some people get special benefits and others special punishments. Such a view of the universe would make one insecure, for whenever he faced a crisis he would be inclined to think of it as punishment.

Similarly, with an inadequate concept of the nature of man, one would be at a disadvantage in coping with crises. If one felt man was a cosmic beggar, inadequate in himself and always needing some special form of cosmic intervention, he would spend his energy trying to manipulate the universe rather than developing his own skills in directing the course of his life. The more healthful view of man would be concerned with understanding his own nature as well as developing the resources for his inner kingdom of being. A person who believes that man is a creature with great and useful endowments will work to develop himself toward fuller adequacy. He will think of himself as little lower than the angels, with great spiritual potential. He will set the highest goals for his life.

The proper study of mankind is man. A person who has fully developed his inner being's resources does not feel separated from the forces of life. He feels as if he is on the inside looking out rather than on the outside looking in. He has made his inner being the impregnable fortress of life. He can really say that he loves whatever happens to him because he is a part of it. His inner being is the focal point of meaning for all existence and in this experience of meaning he finds the perspective that transforms his encounter with life into the opportunity for ever-renewing and ever-growing insight.

We have said little about the social crises of mankind because they are not within the scope of our study. However, we cannot exist as social creatures without being aware of the crises that tend to engulf us all, for ultimately they happen to us individually. Because no one is ever really alone, our personal crises reach others and the social crises filter down into the lives of every individual.

Crises in politics touch the lives of men, women, and children constantly. When a sociopath is elected to high office as in Hitler Germany, the world suffers for generations and people's lives are touched with tragedy and suffering. When there is a paralysis of the basic human values, the crisis touches not only the minorities who are discriminated against but the majorities —who suffer a loss of their inner integrity.

When industry becomes more concerned with things than with people, this callousness is as destructive of the inner meaning of life for those who hold economic power as it is for those who suffer deprivation and abuse.

When discrimination on the basis of sex undermines the rights of any individual, all are embroiled in the social crisis in ways that may not be perceived but that eventually touch everyone—through the atrophy of values.

The larger dimensions of crisis touch us all when there is a breakdown in communication and relationship at the national level, when the nation's resources are employed for the destructiveness of war. When there is a collapse of integrity that paralyzes the useful function of government, those who are least able to defend themselves suffer most immediately but in the long run no one is spared.

Research into the nature of the kind of person most adequate to cope with life shows a quality of concern, a capacity for love, and a depth of awareness of others—the super-healthy person is socially responsive. The clusters of traits that mark individuals with personal adequacy are inevitably social in their reach. These are the virtuous people, concerned about justice and the rights of others, creative in imagination, and filled with a loving outreach. These are the people who can live in the midst of crises with an attitude toward themselves and others that always goes beyond the personal implications of the crisis. Because they understand themselves and others so well, they can move beyond judgments and are concerned primarily with helping and healing.

Just as skill in rational thinking made it possible for developing man to build bridges between the primitive power of his instincts and his acquired wisdom, so the experience of transcendent meaning may make it possible for man to develop to the point where he will be able to live largely above crises and their impact. He will not become hard and heartless and deny his feelings; rather, he will feel so deeply that his feelings will color all of his responses to life. His breadth of love will support the forward movement of life through crisis rather than allowing life to bog him down.

The bridges that we build to greater self-awareness will not be bound with the either-or approach to life. The both-and approach to life will encourage a healthful growth of the self and at the same time a creative concern for others. Cosmic reality will push out the boundaries of experience and growth.

The higher one climbs up the mountainside, the farther he is able to see across the foothills. The inclination to retreat into the valleys of small vision and limiting perspective is strong. But life need not be bound by its littleness. We can climb higher and, as our vistas enlarge, discover a new adequacy within ourselves, and a new appreciation of others.

Eilhard Von Domaris held up a vision of a continuing evolution of man toward a spiritual dimension of being that not only made man at home in the universe but made him feel that he and the universe were partners in working out a personal destiny. Maslow has elaborated on this idea in another context with his concept of a super-healthy individual. Perhaps these super-healthy people have discovered the best ways of coping with the crises of life, for they are able to live above and beyond the destructive impact of crises.

At the beginning of this study we pointed out that people who work in crisis psychology look for the special ingredient that makes it possible for some people to grow through an event successfully, while others are destroyed by it. Certainly many things go into understanding this aspect of human behavior. However, we hope we have created a basis for understanding that will make crises less threatening and make some of the resources for meeting them more accessible.

Ultimately it will be some unmeasurable and intangible grasp of meaning deep within the self that makes it possible to rise above the crises in life and use them for growth rather than let them block growth. It is true that the process of life makes us what we are, but the mastery of life's events makes us something more each time we test our strength.

Each of us is on a private journey through life. We experience events and relationships with other people. Some of us will find the mysterious ingredient that makes crises into stepping-stones. We will discover a self-actualizing principle within ourselves that moves us toward competence and maturity. This growth will not be an easy process; in fact, it may well be the most difficult thing we ever do. It demands that we develop our sense of values. It compels us to be dissatisfied with our escapes and trivialities. It insists that we become truly mature beings.

Each of us must decide for himself whether or not he wants to undergo this process of strenuous self-discipline and growth. But the way is clear. The person who is wise and strong within will not be overwhelmed by anything that comes from without. Through perspective, courage, and growth, he will work to make it good.

BIBLIOGRAPHY

Allport, Gordon W. *Becoming*. New Haven: Yale University Press, 1955.

———. CRM Books Editorial Staff. *Anthropology Today*. Del Mar, Cal.: CRM Books, 1971.

Arnold, Magda B. *The Nature of Emotion*. Baltimore: Penguin Books, 1968.

Bromley, D. B. *The Psychology of Aging*. Baltimore: Penguin Books, 1969.

Caplan, Gerald and Levovici, Serge. *Adolescence: Psychological Perspectives*. New York: Basic Books, 1969.

Caplan, Gerald. *Emotional Problems of Early Childhood*. New York: Science Books, 1955.

Carrel, Alexis, *Man the Unknown*. New York: Harper and Row, 1935.

Drucker, Peter F. *The Age of Discontinuity*. New York: Harper and Row, 1969.

Dunbar, Flanders. *Your Child's Mind and Body*. New York: Random House, 1949.

———. *The Emotions and Bodily Changes*. New York: Columbia University Press, 1954.

Erikson, Erik H. *Childhood and Society*. New York: Norton, 1950.

———. *Insight and Responsibility*. New York: Norton, 1964.

Frankl, Viktor. *The Will to Meaning*. New York: World, 1969.

Fromm, Erich. *Man for Himself*. New York: Holt, Rinehart and Winston, 1947.

Fulton, Robert. *Death and Identity*. New York: John Wiley, 1965.

Gesell Arnold. *The First Five Years of Life*. New York: Harper, 1956.

Gesell, Arnold, and Ilg, Frances L. *The Child from Five to Ten*. New York: Harper and Row, 1946.

Grollman, Earl. *Explaining Death to Children*. Boston: Beacon, 1967.

Horney, Karen. *Our Inner Conflicts*. New York: Norton, 1945.

Johnson, Paul. *The Middle Years*. Philadelphia: Fortress, 1971.

LeShan, Eda. *Sex and Your Teenager*. New York: McKay, 1969.

———. *The Wonderful Crisis of Middle Age*. New York: McKay, 1973.

Madow, Leo. *Anger*. New York: Scribner, 1972

Maslow, Abraham A. *The Farther Reaches of Human Nature.* New York: Viking, 1971.

May, Rollo. *Man's Search for Himself.* New York: Norton, 1953.

Mead, Margaret. *Male and Female.* New York: Morrow, 1949.

Naranjo, Claudio and Ornstein, Robert. *On the Psychology of Meditation.* New York: Viking, 1971.

Parsons, Talcott. *Social Structure and Personality.* Glencoe, Ill.: Free Press, 1965.

Perls, Frederick S. *Ego, Hunger and Aggression.* New York: Random House, 1969.

Rogers, Carl. *On Encounter Groups.* New York: Harper and Row, 1970.

Sheresky, Norman and Mannes, Marya. *Uncoupling.* New York: Viking, 1972.

Simeons, A. T. W. *Man's Presumptuous Brain.* New York: Dutton, 1965.

Toffler, Alvin. *Future Shock.* New York: Random House, 1970.

Tournier, Paul. *The Whole Person in a Broken World.* New York: Harper and Row, 1964.

Wilson, Colin. *New Pathways in Psychology.* New York: Taplinger, 1972

Wolff, Sula. *Children Under Stress.* London: The Penguin Press, 1969.

INDEX